fish indian style ⌐

I WOULD LIKE TO DEDICATE THIS BOOK TO MY FATHER, for being my hero and my guide in the maze of the food world. I lost him earlier this year while writing this book. He was excited about the idea behind the book and wanted so much to see it in print.

Thanks to his sense of seasonality and support for local produce, I learned good things under his umbrella. My first few lessons on professional cookery started in his rustic kitchen and proved to be great building blocks in the years to come. I will miss him tremendously in all seasons – especially when mangoes are in bloom. I feel privileged to have been born his son.

fish indian style

atul kochhar

PHOTOGRAPHY BY
DAVID LOFTUS

ABSOLUTE PRESS

First published in
Great Britain in 2008
by **Absolute Press**
Scarborough House
29 James Street West
Bath BA1 2BT
Phone 44 (0) 1225 316013
Fax 44 (0) 1225 445836
E-mail info@absolutepress.co.uk
Website www.absolutepress.co.uk

Text © Atul Kochhar, 2008
Photography © David Loftus, 2008

Publisher Jon Croft
Commissioning Editor Meg Avent
Art Director Matt Inwood
Editor Jane Middleton
Food Styling Atul Kochhar
Publishing Assistant Andrea O'Connor

A catalogue record of this book is available from the British Library

ISBN 9781904573838
Printed by Printer Trento, Italy

~ contents ~

introduction ~

I have often thought that, despite its long coastline, the Indian subcontinent does not make the most of its seafood. Fish tends to be cooked in 'curries', which mask the qualities that make it special – its colours, textures, flavours and aromas.

In the UK, too, fish cookery is underexploited. It is a country surrounded by vast oceans, yet we shy away from the wealth of seafood available to us – sometimes for free. Although we would all benefit from including fish in our diet more often, many people lack confidence when it comes to buying and cooking fish.

This book aims to come up with a fresher, simpler approach to fish cookery. It unites Indian spicing and techniques with the best of British seafood and other produce, in dishes such as Kentish Oyster Fritters with Cumin and Chilli-Apple Jelly (page 42), Crisp Fried Whiting with Jerusalem Artichokes, Celery and Pears in Curry Vinaigrette (page 69) and Seared Trout with St George's Mushrooms, Radishes and Cheddar Cheese in Garlic and Chilli Dressing (page 71). I have also occasionally drawn on other European culinary traditions – have a look at Mumbai Fish Pizza (page 108), for example, or Seafood Frittata (page 111). Fish is a wonderfully versatile ingredient and, as long as you take care not to overwhelm it, it makes a perfect canvas for spices and herbs. I have discovered that the marriage of British fish and Indian flavours is one of the best there is.

I grew up in East India, where the most inspired Indian fish cookery takes place, amongst communities such as the Bengalis, the Oriyas, the Parsees and the Assamese. My father was extremely proud of his culinary heritage and believed that you should support your local food producers and cook according to the seasons – principles that are now accepted culinary wisdom. When I moved to England, his values came with me, and I immediately started investigating what was available locally. To my delight, I found that I had ended up surrounded by some of the best seafood in the world, from Kentish oysters to scallops from the Isle of Man, from Cromer crab to Scottish herrings.

Surrounded by all this bounty, it would be easy to get carried away but I believe we have to be responsible in our approach to fish cookery, avoiding the highly popular but endangered species, such as cod, tuna and eel, while exploring lesser known but more abundant types, like pollack, signal crayfish and grey mullet. Fish farming can create its own problems but occasionally offers a viable alternative, such as Shetland farmed cod, which is sold under the name Nocatch (www.nocatch.co.uk). For more information on sustainable fish, have a look at the Marine Conservation Society's website, www.fishonline.org, which rates species according to whether stocks are managed in a sustainable fashion.

Indian cooking is often considered complex, and it's true that ingredients lists can be very long. I have tried to ensure that the recipes in this book are simple and accessible – particularly in the chapter on Fish for Everyday (page 82), which focuses on dishes that can be prepared quickly and without fuss. You should be able to find most of the ingredients you need in Asian shops or large supermarkets. If you don't live near any Asian shops, there are now several internet companies providing Indian ingredients by post. I have found Spices of India (www.spicesofindia.co.uk) to be particularly reliable.

Finally, do consider this book as mere guidance, and use your imagination to create new combinations and flavours. Remember, you need to use spices in the same way as salt and pepper in your cooking. Always taste as you go along, and adjust the seasoning as necessary. As you develop your confidence with spices, you will find yourself reaching for your spice box more often. Happy and healthy cooking!

ATUL KOCHHAR London, May 2008

soups & stews ~

mussel soup ⟶

This is one of the easiest soups to make, with the spices adding some dazzling flavours. Crushed coriander seeds and dried chilli provide a lovely textural contrast to the soft flesh of the mussels. The spicing is inspired by the kadhai cooking of northern India, which uses a base of garlic, red chilli flakes and coriander seeds and then rounds the dish off with garam masala. In the UK, this cooking style is known as balti, a name that mistakenly evolved here for the kadhai, which is a kind of Indian wok.

Alternative fish
any shellfish

SERVES 6-8

2kg mussels
150ml dry white wine
1 tablespoon vegetable oil
2 garlic cloves, finely chopped
¼ teaspoon crushed coriander seeds
¼ teaspoon red chilli flakes
1 small onion, finely chopped
2cm piece of fresh ginger, finely
   chopped
½ teaspoon ground turmeric
½ teaspoon garam masala
450ml Saffron Fish Stock (see page 203)
150ml double cream
juice of ½ lime
1 tablespoon chopped dill or tarragon
sea salt and freshly ground black
   pepper

Scrub the mussels under cold running water, pulling out the beards and discarding any open mussels that don't close when tapped on the work surface. Place the mussels in a large pan and pour over the wine. Cover with a tight-fitting lid and cook over a fairly high heat for 5 minutes or so, shaking the pan occasionally, until the shells open. Strain the mussel cooking liquid through a fine sieve into a clean bowl and set aside.

Heat the oil in a large pan, add the garlic, coriander seeds and chilli and sauté gently until soft and golden. Add the onion and sauté until translucent. Stir in the ginger, turmeric and garam masala, plus the saffron stock and strained mussel cooking liquid, and simmer gently for 10 minutes. Meanwhile, shell the mussels, setting aside about 20 unshelled ones as a garnish. Discard any mussels that haven't opened.

Stir the shelled mussels and the cream into the soup, add a squeeze of lime juice and season to taste. Heat through gently, stir in the dill or tarragon, then ladle into bowls. Divide the reserved mussels between the bowls and serve.

citrus langoustine soup ~

JHINGAE KA SHORBA

I created this light, delicate soup as an experiment to serve as a pre-starter at Benares. It was so popular that people asked for second helpings.

Once you have cooked the langoustines, I recommend using the shells to make the stock (see page 203). Langoustines are sometimes labelled Dublin Bay prawns. If you find any soft, creamy matter (the tomalley, or liver) in the heads when cleaning them, don't throw it away. You can scoop it out with a spoon and add it to the soup.

Alternative fish
prawns

SERVES 4

300g raw langoustines
1 tablespoon sunflower oil
1 lemongrass stalk, tough outer layers removed, then finely chopped
2 tablespoons finely chopped fresh ginger
1 garlic clove, chopped
1 onion, thinly sliced
¼ teaspoon ground turmeric
¼ teaspoon dried mango powder
1 large red chilli, deseeded and sliced
1 tablespoon palm sugar
1 tablespoon tamarind pulp (see page 218) or tomato paste
1 litre fish or shellfish stock (see page 203) or chicken stock
juice and grated zest of 2 limes
2 spring onions, cut into fine strips
1 large green mango, peeled, stoned and cut into fine strips
3 tablespoons fresh or frozen peas
1 teaspoon coriander seeds, toasted in a dry frying pan and then crushed
1 tablespoon finely chopped coriander leaves
1 tablespoon shredded purple or green basil
sea salt and freshly ground black pepper

Add the langoustines to a large pan of boiling salted water, bring back to the boil and simmer for 3–4 minutes, Drain, refresh in cold water and drain again, then peel off the shells. Set the langoustine flesh aside.

Heat the oil in a large pan, add the lemongrass, ginger and garlic and sauté for 1–2 minutes, until slightly softened. Add the onion and sauté for 2 minutes or until translucent. Stir in the turmeric and dried mango powder, followed by the sliced red chilli, palm sugar and tamarind pulp. Pour in the stock, bring to the boil and simmer for 10 minutes. Add the lime juice and zest. Simmer for 4–5 minutes, then add the langoustines, spring onions, mango, peas, crushed coriander seeds, chopped coriander and basil. Correct the seasoning with salt and pepper and serve at once.

COCONUT AND fENNEL SOUP WITH *seareD* MONKfISH

SAUNF AU NARIYAL KA SHORBA

This recipe sounds very posh but actually it's not at all difficult to make. It takes its inspiration from the Mangalore region of India, where the use of fennel and star anise is very common.

Fresh coconuts can be difficult to find in the UK, so by all means go for canned or frozen coconut cream instead – it won't be a sin.

Alternative fish
pollack, whiting, hake

SERVES 4

2 tablespoons vegetable oil
1 onion, finely chopped
2 star anise
1 teaspoon fennel seeds
100ml white wine
500ml fish stock (see page 203)
500ml coconut milk
50ml double cream
200g monkfish tail, cut into 4 pieces
olive oil for drizzling
sea salt and freshly ground black pepper

To garnish
½ teaspoon fennel seeds, toasted in a dry frying pan and then crushed
a small pinch of saffron strands
1 tablespoon finely chopped dill

Heat the oil in a pan, add the onion, star anise and fennel seeds and sauté for 5–8 minutes, until the onion is soft and translucent. Add the white wine and simmer for about 5 minutes, until reduced by half. Add the fish stock, bring to the boil and simmer gently for 20 minutes, then add the coconut milk and cook for a further 10 minutes.

Remove the pan from the heat and take out the star anise. Purée the soup in a blender or food processor until smooth, then pass it through a fine sieve into a clean pan, rubbing with the back of a ladle or a wooden spoon to push as much through the sieve as possible. Season to taste and reheat gently. Stir in the double cream and keep warm.

Season the monkfish tail and drizzle with olive oil. Sear it on all sides in a hot, heavy-based non-stick frying pan until it is a good golden colour; this should not take more than 2 minutes per side. Remove from the heat and leave to rest for 5 minutes, then cut each piece into 2–3 slices.

Ladle the soup into warmed soup plates and place the seared monkfish tail in the centre. Sprinkle the toasted fennel seeds, saffron strands and dill on top and serve immediately.

'This is really a
summery recipe but is
great at other times of year as well.'

WATERCRESS SOUP WITH SALMON KOFTA ─

THANDA HARA SHORBA AUR MACHCHI KE KOFTE

This is really a summery recipe but is great at other times of year as well. Watercress lends its characteristic sharpness to the soup.

SERVES 2

Alternative fish
cod, rainbow trout, sea trout

1 tablespoon vegetable or sunflower oil
1 tablespoon butter
1 small onion, diced
200g watercress, tough stalks removed
300ml vegetable stock
100ml double cream, plus a little extra to garnish
2 tablespoons chopped mint
sea salt and freshly ground black pepper
beet cress, if available, to garnish (or use mustard cress or torn radicchio leaves)

For the salmon kofta
1 tablespoon vegetable oil
½ teaspoon mustard seeds
2 curry leaves
¼ teaspoon grated fresh ginger
2 tablespoons finely chopped shallots or onion
200g salmon fillet, skinned, pin bones removed
1 egg white
1 tablespoon single cream
½ teaspoon finely grated orange zest
4 walnuts, lightly toasted in a dry frying pan and then crushed
leaves from a sprig of lemon thyme
light stock for poaching (optional)

Melt the oil and butter in a medium saucepan, add the onion and sauté until soft. Add the watercress and let it wilt, then pour in the stock. Bring to the boil, reduce the heat and simmer for 4 minutes. Transfer the soup to a food processor or blender and blitz until smooth. Return the soup to the pan, add the cream and simmer for 2 minutes. Stir in the mint and remove from the heat. Season to taste.

To make the kofta, heat the oil in a small pan, add the mustard seeds and sauté for a minute, then add the curry leaves, ginger and shallots. Sauté for about 2 minutes, until the shallots are lightly cooked, then remove from the heat and leave to cool. Mince the salmon fillet finely. You can use a food processor for this, as long as you pulse it rather than letting the machine run, or you can chop it very finely with a large, sharp knife. Mix the minced salmon with the egg white, cream, orange zest, walnuts and thyme leaves, then lightly stir in the sautéed shallot mixture and some salt and pepper. Shape the mixture into walnut-sized balls. Add them to a pan of gently simmering stock or water and poach for 3–4 minutes, until just set. Remove with a slotted spoon and drain on kitchen paper.

Reheat the soup if necessary and pour it into serving bowls. Lightly drop in the kofta (3–4 per person). Garnish the soup with beet cress, if available, and a swirl of cream.

officers' club mulligatawny

Mulligatawny is a Tamil term, meaning pepper water. The soup was adapted by Indian cooks in charge of the British officers' mess during the Raj. To suit the British palate, they made it creamier and a little sweeter.

Traditionally, mulligatawny is either vegetarian or made with chicken stock but there are many fish versions too, including some with smoked haddock and some with dried prawns. I like to make a fish version, and am particularly fond of this one with crab.

SERVES 4

2 tablespoons sunflower or olive oil
1 onion, chopped
1 carrot, chopped
10 curry leaves or 1 bay leaf
1½ teaspoons Ginger Paste
  (see page 202)
1½ teaspoons Garlic Paste
  (see page 202)
1 large cooked crab, still in the shell,
  roughly chopped (you could ask
  your fishmonger to do this)
1 tablespoon gram flour, lightly
  toasted in a dry frying pan
1½ teaspoons mild curry powder
2 Granny Smith apples, peeled, cored
  and sliced
2 plum tomatoes, chopped
1 litre fish stock (see page 203)
sea salt

To serve
4 tablespoons single cream
¼ teaspoon crushed black pepper
1 tablespoon lemon juice
2 tablespoons cooked basmati rice
2 tablespoons peeled and finely
  chopped Granny Smith apple
1 tablespoon finely chopped
  coriander leaves

Heat the oil in a large pan, add the onion, carrot and curry leaves or bay leaf and sauté for 3–4 minutes, until softened. Add the ginger and garlic paste, sauté for 2–3 minutes to cook through and then add the crab pieces and sauté for another 2–3 minutes. Stir in the gram flour and curry powder, sauté for 2 minutes, then add the sliced apples, tomatoes and fish stock. Bring to the boil and simmer for 25–30 minutes.

Remove from the heat and cool slightly. Take out the pieces of crab, wrap them in a cloth and bash with a hammer or rolling pin until broken into tiny pieces. Return all the bits to the soup, then strain through a conical sieve. Finally, strain it again through a really fine sieve.

Return the soup to the pan, bring to the boil and simmer until slightly reduced. Season to taste with salt. Stir in the cream, crushed black pepper, lemon juice, cooked rice and apple, then finish with the chopped coriander. Serve straight away.

calcutta fish stew

MACHER JHOL

Bengalis are renowned for their love of fish. Like the people of the Mediterranean, they are passionate about good, fresh food. I ate a lot of Bengali food as a child and then while working for the Oberoi hotel group, but the meals I remember most are the ones I ate in Calcutta. There is a lovely restaurant there called Kewpie, which was originally owned by the late Minakshie das Gupta, a highly talented cook. I wasn't fortunate enough to eat there in her time but her family continues to do an impeccable job and honour her culinary principles. This dish is made in every home in Bengal, but the version served at Kewpie is the best and the inspiration for this recipe.

Alternative fish
sea bass, grey mullet, red gurnard, brill

SERVES 4

2 tablespoons vegetable oil
1 teaspoon panch phoran (see page 217)
1 bay leaf
1 dried red chilli
½ teaspoon finely chopped fresh ginger
1 onion, sliced
100g Jersey Royal potatoes (or other waxy potatoes), sliced
1 tomato, sliced
100g carrots, finely sliced
100g yellow pumpkin, peeled and finely sliced
100g cauliflower, cut into small florets
50g green cabbage, thinly sliced
½ teaspoon ground turmeric
½ teaspoon ground coriander
½ teaspoon chilli powder
½ teaspoon ground cumin
400ml fish stock (see page 203)
½ teaspoon sugar
sea salt
a few sprigs of chervil or coriander, to garnish

To cook the fish
½ teaspoon fennel seeds
½ teaspoon coriander seeds
½ teaspoon black sesame seeds
4 x 100g turbot steaks
1 tablespoon vegetable oil
1 tablespoon butter

Heat the oil in a large pan over a medium heat and add the panch phoran, bay leaf and dried chilli. As they crackle, add the ginger and sauté for 1 minute. Add the onion and sauté for 2–3 minutes, then stir in all the vegetables and sauté for 3–5 minutes. Stir in all the ground spices, sauté for 1–2 minutes and then add the fish stock, sugar and some salt. Cook until the vegetables are completely tender. Remove from the heat and keep warm.

To cook the fish, sprinkle the seeds over the turbot steaks. Heat the oil in a non-stick pan, add the turbot and fry over a medium heat for 1–2 minutes on each side. Just before finishing, add the butter to the pan, let it melt, then spoon it over the fish.

Pour the stew into deep plates and place the fish on top. Garnish with chervil or coriander sprigs and serve.

NORTH INDIAN-STYLE STEW of FARMED COD ~

MACHCHI KA SHORBA

I was introduced to cod in the UK and loved it right from the start. Slowly I came to realise that stocks were being depleted but, as luck would have it, cod farming was set up in Shetland about four years ago. I always use farmed cod in my cooking now. The quality is excellent and my conscience is clear. In this particular recipe I've given the fish a north Indian treatment. It's a perfect dish for a hot summer's day – just serve with good bread to soak up the juices.

Alternative fish
pollack, whiting, ling

SERVES 4

2 tablespoons vegetable oil
¼ teaspoon cumin seeds
½ green chilli, finely chopped
¼ teaspoon finely chopped fresh
   ginger
1 onion, sliced
1 medium potato, peeled, sliced and
   boiled until just tender
½ teaspoon ground turmeric
½ teaspoon ground coriander
1 tablespoon tomato purée
500ml fish stock (see page 203)
2 tomatoes, skinned and diced
1 tablespoon chopped coriander
   leaves
a small pinch of garam masala
4 x 100g pieces of farmed Shetland
   cod fillet
1 tablespoon butter
sea salt
a small bunch of coriander cress (or
   sprigs of coriander), to garnish

Heat half the oil in a large pan, add the cumin seeds, green chilli and ginger and sauté over a medium heat until the cumin starts to crackle. Add the onion and sauté for 3–5 minutes, until translucent. Add the potato and half the ground turmeric and coriander and cook for a couple of minutes. Stir in the tomato purée and cook for 2–3 minutes, then add the fish stock. Bring to the boil, simmer for 5–7 minutes and then add the tomatoes. Simmer on a low heat for 3–4 minutes. Sprinkle with the chopped coriander and the garam masala.

Meanwhile, season the fish fillets with salt and sprinkle on the remaining turmeric and ground coriander. Heat the remaining tablespoon of oil in a frying pan, add the fish and fry over a medium heat until lightly coloured on both sides and just cooked through. Add the butter to the pan, let it melt, then spoon it over the fish.

To serve, pour the stew into deep plates and place a piece of fried fish on top. Garnish with the coriander cress or sprigs.

goan shellfish stew

MA GOA ISTEW

Goa is a unique blend of East and West. I have enjoyed its culture and hospitality numerous times and its food has always been special to me. Walking along its beautiful beaches, I often think it must be an ideal place to live – not least because so many wonderful fish are landed there. This stew is similar to the ones fishermen's wives make from any leftover catch they haven't sold in the market. It is a fresh and delicious dish that can be created with whatever you can get from your local fishmonger – the shellfish listed below are just suggestions.

SERVES 4

600g mussels
600g cockles
1 tablespoon vegetable oil
1 tablespoon finely chopped fresh
  ginger
200ml coconut milk
200ml fish stock (see page 203)
2 tablespoons chopped coriander
  leaves

For the spice paste
1 tablespoon coriander seeds
1½ teaspoons cumin seeds
½ teaspoon cloves
¼ teaspoon black peppercorns
1 small dried red chilli
8 garlic cloves, peeled
1 teaspoon ground turmeric
½ teaspoon ground coriander
1 tablespoon tamarind pulp (see page
  218) or lemon juice
2 onions, roughly chopped

2 tablespoons coconut vinegar
  or white wine vinegar
50ml coconut cream

First make the spice paste. Put the coriander, cumin, cloves, peppercorns and red chilli in a heavy-based frying pan and toast them over a medium heat for a few minutes, shaking the pan occasionally, until they are aromatic. Leave to cool and then grind to a fine powder in a spice mill or coffee grinder. Put this spice powder in a food processor with the rest of the ingredients and blend to a fine paste. Set aside until required.

Scrub the mussels and clams under cold running water, discarding any open ones that don't close when tapped on the work surface. Pull out and discard the beards from the mussels.

Heat the oil in a wok, add the ginger and sauté over a medium heat for about a minute, until lightly caramelised. Add the spice paste and sauté until the oil starts separating out from it. Add the shellfish and cook over a high heat for 3–4 minutes, until the shells open. Stir in the coconut milk and stock and simmer for 2–3 minutes. Remove from the heat and sprinkle with the chopped coriander. Serve hot, with naan bread.

starters ~

CRISP fRiED wHITEBAIt ~

In the Bombay (now Mumbai) region of western India, *bombil,* or Bombay duck, is a favourite snack among fish eaters. Deep-fried, with a light coating of flour and spices, it was also very popular with the British during colonial times – perhaps because it reminded them of the English dish of deep-fried whitebait. Famously, Bombay duck is nothing to do with duck but is in fact *Harpadon nehereus,* or lizardfish. It can be eaten fresh but is often sold salted and dried. For this recipe you will probably have to use frozen whitebait, since it is rarely available fresh.

SERVES 4

300g whitebait
2 tablespoons lemon juice
1 tablespoon Ginger-Garlic Paste (see page 202)
1 teaspoon ground turmeric
1 teaspoon red chilli powder
100g rice flour
100g fine semolina
sunflower oil for deep-frying
Spicy Tomato Chutney (see page 206) or Onion Raita (see page 211) and lemon wedges, to serve

Wash the fish under cold running water and pat dry on kitchen paper. Mix together the lemon juice, ginger-garlic paste, turmeric and chilli powder. Rub this paste on the fish and set aside for 10 minutes.

Mix the rice flour and semolina together in a bowl, add the fish and toss well to coat. Transfer the fish to a sieve and shake to get rid of excess flour.

Heat the sunflower oil to 180°C in a deep-fat fryer or a large, deep saucepan. Fry the whitebait in the hot oil, in batches if necessary, for 2–3 minutes, until crisp and light golden. Drain on kitchen paper and serve straight away, with the chutney or raita and lemon wedges.

'Tawa cooking can be a fascinating piece
of theatre. The food sizzles away on
the griddle, seasoned with a
generous amount of spicing.'

crisp sardines —

TAWAE KI MACHCHI

There are three types of grilling in India: in a tandoor (a charcoal-fired oven), on a *sigri*, or *sinkri* (an open barbecue or grill) and on a *tawa* (a flat griddle). Tawa cooking can be a fascinating piece of theatre. The food sizzles away on the griddle, seasoned with a generous amount of spicing. This recipe uses southern Indian flavours rather than traditional tawa spicing, but it works really well.

Alternative fish
any small fish

SERVES 4

8 sardine fillets
1½ teaspoons sambhar powder
  (or curry powder)
2 tablespoons vegetable oil
1 teaspoon lime juice
sea salt
mixed cress or sprigs of herbs, to garnish
Tomato-Ginger Chutney (see page 208),
  to serve

Dust the sardine fillets with the sambhar powder and some salt. Heat the oil in a heavy-based frying pan or on a flat griddle, add the sardine fillets, skin-side down, and fry over a medium-high heat for 2 minutes. Turn and cook the other side for 1 minute, until the fish is just done. Sprinkle over the lime juice. Transfer to 4 serving plates, garnish with cress or herb sprigs, and serve with the chutney.

south indian-style
fish roes ~

Fish roes are cooked in various ways in South India – curried, sautéed, deep-fried, etc. I have adapted this recipe to suit herring roes, which are readily available in the UK. The spice paste is very versatile and can be used with prawns, mussels or any small fish.

SERVES 4

500g herring roes
2 tablespoons lime juice
3 tablespoons sunflower oil
1 lemongrass stalk, lightly bruised
5 curry leaves
150ml coconut milk
1 red chilli, sliced
sea salt

For the spice paste
2 dried red chillies
1 teaspoon coriander seeds
¼ teaspoon fennel seeds, toasted in a
  dry frying pan
½ teaspoon cumin seeds
1 tablespoon desiccated coconut
½ tablespoon dried mango powder
1 tablespoon finely chopped fresh
  ginger
1 teaspoon ground turmeric
2 garlic cloves, chopped
4 shallots, sliced
½ teaspoon sea salt

To serve
coriander cress or sprigs of coriander
4 slices of bread, toasted and buttered
4 slices of lime

Mix the herring roes with the lime juice and a sprinkling of salt and leave in the fridge for 10 minutes.

Put all the ingredients for the spice paste in a blender with 2 tablespoons of water and blend until smooth. Mix the spice paste with the roes. Heat the sunflower oil in a large frying pan, add the roes and sauté for 2 minutes over a medium heat. Add the bruised lemon grass stalk and the curry leaves and sauté for 2 minutes, then add the coconut milk and sliced chilli. Cook over a low heat for 3–5 minutes, until the roes are firm to the touch and lightly coated in the sauce. Serve hot on buttered toast, garnished with coriander cress or sprigs and a slice of lime.

goan *fish* rolls —

FOFOS

This dish is a legacy of the Portuguese occupation of Goa, when ingredients such as bread, cheese and vinegar became assimilated into the cuisine and the locals picked up European cooking techniques. Originally it was made with salt cod, but over time the dried fish has been replaced by fresh. The rolls make an enjoyable party snack and the recipe can be adapted to prawns as well.

SERVES 4

500g white fish fillets
about 500ml fish stock (see page 203)
2 eggs, separated
1 red onion, finely chopped
1 potato, boiled until tender, then peeled and grated
1 green chilli, finely chopped
1 tablespoon finely chopped fresh ginger
1 teaspoon cumin seeds, toasted in a dry frying pan
1 tablespoon chopped coriander leaves
1 tablespoon cornflour
6 tablespoons fresh breadcrumbs
sunflower oil for deep-frying
sea salt and freshly ground black pepper
Spicy Tomato Chutney (see page 206), to serve

Put the fish fillets in a pan in a single layer, pour over enough fish stock to cover and bring slowly to a simmer. Cook gently for 2–3 minutes, until the fish is just done, then remove the fish from the liquid and leave to cool. Flake the fish, removing any skin and bones, then put it in a bowl with the egg yolks, onion, grated potato, chilli, ginger, cumin, coriander and cornflour. Add 50ml of the fish poaching liquid, mix well and season to taste. Divide the mixture into 16 pieces and shape them into croquettes.

Lightly beat the egg whites together in a small bowl. Put the breadcrumbs in another bowl, then dip the croquettes into the egg white and roll them in the breadcrumbs until completely coated. Leave the croquettes to rest in the fridge for 10–15 minutes.

Heat the oil to 180°C in a deep-fat fryer or a large, deep saucepan. Fry the croquettes in batches for 1–2 minutes, until they are light golden. Drain on kitchen paper and serve hot, accompanied by the chutney.

FISH – INDIAN STYLE

indian-style escabeche of mackerel

Escabeche is a Spanish dish but the liberal use of spices has prompted me to make my own version. Sardines are the classic fish to use but mackerel works very well, too.

SERVES 4–6

8 small mackerel fillets
2 tablespoons sambhar powder (or good curry powder)
2 tablespoons sunflower oil

For the marinade
3 tablespoons sunflower oil
2 teaspoons panch phoran (see page 217)
1 dried red chilli
2 garlic cloves, sliced
2 bay leaves
5 shallots, sliced
3 carrots, sliced
2 baby fennel bulbs, sliced
100ml white wine
50ml white wine vinegar
½ teaspoon sea salt
1 teaspoon sugar
2 tablespoons chopped coriander leaves

Dust the mackerel fillets with the sambhar powder. Heat the oil in a large frying pan, add the mackerel fillets and fry over a medium-high heat on both sides until just lightly coloured. Place them in a warmed shallow terracotta, china or glass dish; the fish should fit in it in a single layer.

For the marinade, heat the oil in a pan, add the panch phoran and the red chilli and sauté over a medium heat until the spices begin to pop. Add the garlic and bay leaves, cook until the garlic is lightly coloured, then add the shallots, carrots and fennel. Cook until the shallots are soft and translucent. Add the white wine, vinegar, salt and sugar. Simmer for 5 minutes and then pour the marinade over the fried fish. Sprinkle on the coriander and cover the dish with a tight-fitting lid or with cling film. Leave to cool and then store in the fridge overnight. It is best served at room temperature, so remove the dish from the fridge about 2 hours before you want to eat. Serve with naan, roti or any other flatbread, for mopping up the juices.

sea TROUT ceviche ⁓

Indians will eat anything but raw fish. I have a tough time explaining to them that the fish in this dish effectively cooks in the marinade, thanks to the action of the acid in the lime juice. But I do believe a cuisine has to grow and bring in more influences to expand the repertoire. This is an inspired recipe and it works wonders. The technique is given different names across the world – ceviche in Latin America, *kelaguen* in the Mariana Islands and kinilaw or *kilawin* in the Philippines. The principle of marinating raw fish is the same in all these places.

Alternative fish
salmon, lemon sole, brill, monkfish, sea
  bass, mackerel, pollack, cod, scallops

SERVES 4

400g sea trout fillet, skinned
juice of 3 limes (or 3 tablespoons
  coconut vinegar)
½ tablespoon coconut oil or
  sunflower oil
1 small onion, finely sliced
1 small red chilli, deseeded and finely
  sliced
1 small green chilli, deseeded and
  finely sliced
½ teaspoon cumin seeds, toasted in a
  dry frying pan and then ground to
  a powder
a small pinch of garam masala
1 small green mango, peeled, stoned
  and cut into thin strips
½ teaspoon palm sugar
1 tablespoon finely chopped
  coriander leaves
sea salt

Remove any bones from the fish and then slice it across the grain into strips 1cm thick. Put them in a ceramic, glass or plastic container (don't use metal, which will taint the flavour). Mix the lime juice, oil, onion, chillies, cumin, garam masala, mango, palm sugar and a pinch of salt together. Mix carefully with the fish. Leave to marinate in the fridge for at least 1 hour (but no more than 10 hours). The fish will 'cook' in the marinade and turn opaque.

Correct the seasoning to taste and stir in the chopped coriander. Serve in chilled small, deep bowls with some of the marinating juices.

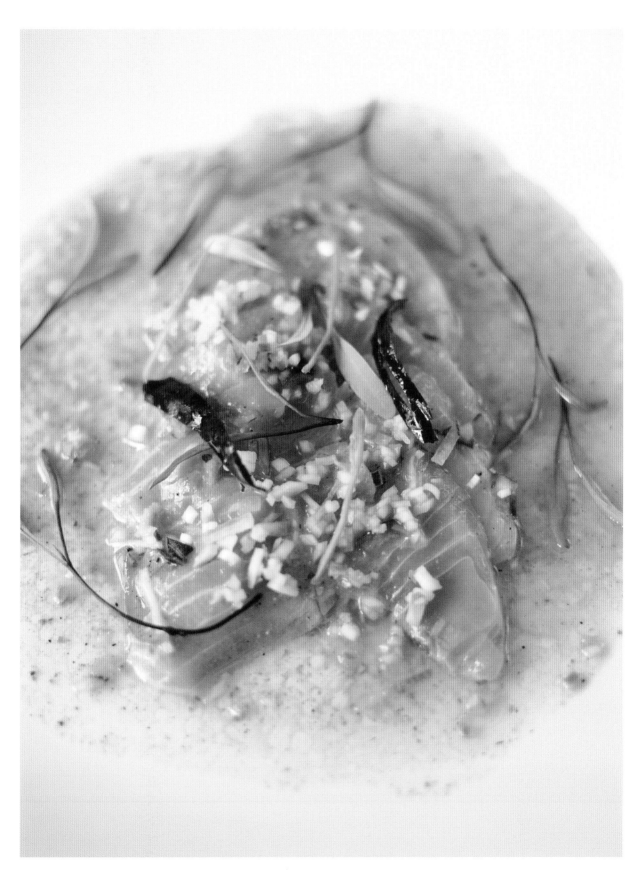

indian-style gravad lax with blini

This is my Indian version of the classic Scandanavian dish, gravad lax. It's very simple to prepare and pleases everyone.

SERVES 6–8

Alternative fish
sea trout, or even a white fish for adventurous cooks!

1kg salmon fillet, in a piece
1 teaspoon honey mixed with
   1 teaspoon English mustard
2 tablespoons finely chopped
   coriander leaves
thick yoghurt, to serve

For the marinade
70g coarse salt
70g caster sugar
juice and zest of 1 orange
½ teaspoon garam masala
juice and zest of 2 limes
1½ teaspoons coriander seeds
a small bunch of coriander roots

For the blini
100g gram flour
150ml carbonated water
sea salt and freshly ground black
   pepper

Mix all the ingredients for the marinade together and rub them on to the flesh side of the fish. Wrap the fish and its marinade tightly in cling film, put it in a dish and leave in the fridge for 24 hours, turning it over every 6 hours or so.

Unwrap the fish, wash it under a cold running tap, then carefully wipe dry. Brush with the honey and mustard mixture and pat the coriander on top. Leave to rest for 1 hour.

For the blini, put the flour in a bowl with some salt and pepper and whisk in enough carbonated water to give a smooth, thick batter with a dropping consistency. Heat a lightly oiled, heavy-based frying pan (preferably non-stick) and drop in small spoonfuls of the batter. Cook over a medium heat for about 1 minute per side, until lightly coloured.

Slice the salmon thinly on the diagonal and serve with the blini and a spoonful of thick yoghurt.

salmon brochettes marinated in mustard and honey ~

TAWAE KE MACHCHI KEBAB

Salmon has a lovely texture, and its brilliant flavour prompts cooks to create some great combinations. I have used really easy spicing here to let the salmon do the talking.

Alternative fish
swordfish, monkfish

SERVES 4

400g salmon fillet, skinned and cut into 3cm cubes
1 red and 1 green pepper, cut into 3cm squares
1 red onion, cut into 3cm squares
30g butter, melted
1 tablespoon finely chopped coriander leaves
1 teaspoon chaat masala
1 lemon, cut into wedges
Onion Raita (see page 211), to serve

For the tikka marinade
250g Greek-style yoghurt
1 tablespoon Ginger-Garlic Paste (see page 202)
1 tablespoon lemon juice
1 tablespoon Dijon mustard
1 tablespoon honey
1 tablespoon ajwain seeds
1 teaspoon black peppercorns, coarsely crushed
1 teaspoon ground coriander
½ teaspoon red chilli powder
½ teaspoon garam masala
½ teaspoon ground turmeric, or a few strands of saffron
1 tablespoon finely chopped fresh ginger
1 tablespoon tomato paste (optional)
sea salt

Mix all the ingredients for the marinade together and set aside in a non-metallic container in the fridge for 20 minutes. Add the fish, peppers and onion to the marinade and leave in the fridge for 1–2 hours.

Thread 2–3 pieces of fish each on 4 metal skewers (or wooden ones that have been soaked in cold water for an hour), alternating the fish with the peppers and onion. Heat a well-oiled griddle or a barbecue, add the fish and cook for about 12 minutes on each side, until lightly coloured. The fish should be firm and opaque when cooked. Brush with the melted butter, then sprinkle with the chopped coriander and chaat masala. Serve with the raita and lemon wedges on the side.

FISH – INDIAN STYLE

pollack cakes —

MACHCHI KI TIKKI

Thai fishcakes have become very popular in the West in recent years but ones prepared with Indian flavours are excellent, too. Lime and lemon work very well in fishcakes, so if you are fond of that citrus kick, use them liberally – include a little grated lime zest for extra punch, if you like.

SERVES 4

300g potatoes, peeled and cut into
   chunks
a small bunch of coriander, including
   the roots
500ml milk
500ml coconut milk
2.5cm piece of fresh ginger, smashed
600g pollack fillet
1 teaspoon ajwain seeds
2 teaspoons chaat masala
juice of 1 lime
vegetable oil for shallow-frying
sea salt
Mint and Coriander Chutney
   (see page 207), to serve

Cook the potatoes in boiling salted water until tender, then drain well. Mash thoroughly and leave to cool.

Meanwhile, separate the coriander leaves from the stalks, chop them and set aside. Chop the roots and stalks roughly. Put the milk, coconut milk, ginger and coriander roots and stalks in a pan and bring just to a simmer. Add the pollack and take off the heat straight away. Cover and leave to stand for 10 minutes. Drain the fish (you won't need the poaching liquid) and leave to cool. Flake the flesh, discarding the skin and any bones.

Mix the fish with the mashed potato, ajwain seeds, chaat masala, lime juice, coriander leaves and some salt. Shape into cakes about 4–5cm in diameter and chill for 30 minutes.

Heat a thin layer of vegetable oil in a large frying pan and fry the cakes until golden brown and crisp on both sides. Serve with the chutney.

.

whiting goujons with onion raita ⁓

Most of us feel a certain amount of nostalgia for fish fingers. As I grew up in India, mine were spicy. I remember my Dad used to make them with cumin, ajwain and coriander.

Alternative fish
pollack, cod, salmon

SERVES 4

400g whiting fillet, skinned
1 tablespoon Ginger-Garlic Paste (see page 202)
¼ teaspoon red chilli powder or paprika
¼ teaspoon ground turmeric
¼ teaspoon coriander seeds, toasted in a dry frying pan and then crushed
1 tablespoon chopped coriander leaves, plus a few leaves to garnish
2 teaspoons finely chopped fresh ginger
1 teaspoon lemon juice
1 teaspoon finely grated lemon zest
2 eggs, lightly beaten
200g fresh breadcrumbs
vegetable oil for deep-frying
sea salt
Onion Raita (see page 211), to serve

Cut the whiting fillet into goujons (fingers). Mix the ginger-garlic paste with the chilli powder, turmeric, coriander seeds and leaves, ginger, lemon juice and zest and some salt. Mix this marinade with the whiting fingers and leave to marinate for 20–30 minutes.

Put the beaten eggs in a bowl and the breadcrumbs in another. Holding a goujon in one hand, dip it in the beaten egg, then with the other hand roll it over in the breadcrumbs, patting lightly to press them on. Repeat with the remaining goujons, then leave them to rest in the fridge for 15–20 minutes.

Heat the oil to 180–190°C in a deep-fat fryer or a large deep pan. Drop the goujons into the hot oil, cooking them in small batches to get the best result. Fry for 2–3 minutes, until light golden, then remove and drain on on kitchen paper.

Serve the goujons hot, garnished with coriander leaves and accompanied by the raita.

FISH - INDIAN STYLE

squid salad with passion fruit and sweet chilli sauce

TALELI MAKALI

Squid is one fish that is actually better frozen. After thawing, the protein in the squid relaxes, making it far more of a delight to eat than the fresh fish, which can be rubbery.

SERVES 4

500g squid rings
juice of 1 lime
2 tablespoons rice flour (ground rice)
2 tablespoons cornflour
1 tablespoon red chilli powder
20g Ginger-Garlic Paste (see page 202)
2 teaspoons chaat masala
vegetable oil for deep-frying
sea salt

To serve
4 handfuls of colourful salad leaves
Passion Fruit and Sweet Chilli Sauce
  (see page 208)

Toss the squid rings with the lime juice and set aside. In a large bowl, mix together all the remaining ingredients except the oil. Add the squid and mix well with your hands, so the squid is lightly coated in the seasonings.

Heat some vegetable oil to 180°C in a deep-fat fryer or a large, deep saucepan and deep-fry the squid in batches for 1–1½ minutes, until golden. Drain on kitchen paper, toss with the salad leaves and drizzle with the sauce. Serve straight away.

kentish oyster fritters with cumin and chilli-apple jelly

I was introduced to Kentish oysters by Gary Rhodes, when I was competing against him on the *Great British Menu* BBC television series. They are particularly plump and succulent, and hold their natural juices well. When I cooked them in this simple cumin-scented batter, the results were stunning. If you can't get Kentish oysters, Pacific or any other fresh oysters are fine.

SERVES 4

16–20 Kentish oysters
vegetable oil for deep-frying

For the chilli-apple jelly
2 gelatine leaves
500ml clear apple juice
1 teaspoon red chilli flakes

For the batter
4 tablespoons gram flour
1½ tablespoons cornflour
1 teaspoon cumin seeds, lightly
   toasted in a dry frying pan
¼ teaspoon red chilli flakes or
   coarsely ground black pepper
1 teaspoon finely grated lime zest
1 tablespoon lime juice
50–100ml sparkling water
sea salt

First make the jelly. Soak the gelatine leaves in cold water for about 5 minutes. Warm the apple juice until hand hot. Squeeze out excess water from the gelatine leaves and add them to the juice, stirring until dissolved. Stir in the chilli flakes and pour the mixture into a baking tray lined with cling film. Leave to cool, then chill until set.

To open the oysters, you will need an oyster knife or any short, sturdy knife. With your hand wrapped in a cloth to protect it, take an oyster and insert the knife blade between the shells, next to the hinge. Twist the knife to lever up the top shell, then cut the muscle connecting the oyster to the shell. Loosen the muscle connecting the oyster to the bottom shell and remove the oyster. Strain the juices through a fine sieve into a bowl and set aside.

Heat the oil to 190°C in a deep-fat fryer or a large, deep saucepan and maintain it at this temperature. Whisk all the ingredients for the batter together, adding the juices from the oysters and enough sparkling water to give a pouring consistency. Dip the oysters into the batter one by one and drop them into the hot oil. Fry for 1–2 minutes, until crisp and pale golden. Drain on kitchen paper and serve hot, with a spoonful of the chilli-apple jelly.

prawn poori ⌐

This is a genuine 'made in England' recipe from the 1960s – it simply doesn't exist in India. The first time I ate it was at Khan's restaurant in Bayswater. It was so good that I later created my own version.

Alternative fish
crayfish, shrimps, langoustines

SERVES 4

20 medium prawns
2 tablespoons vegetable oil
½ teaspoon ajwain or cumin seeds
1 onion, finely chopped
¼ teaspoon ground turmeric
¼ teaspoon red chilli powder or mild paprika
¼ teaspoon garam masala
2 tablespoons chopped peppers (a mixture of green, yellow and red)
1 teaspoon finely chopped fresh ginger
2 tomatoes, chopped
1½ teaspoons lemon juice
1 tablespoon chopped coriander leaves
4 large Pooris (see page 215)
sea salt

To serve
Mint and Coriander Chutney (see page 207)
Tamarind Chutney (see page 207)
Sweet Yoghurt Chutney (see page 209)
sprigs of coriander

Peel the prawns and, using the point of a sharp knife, remove the dark, intestinal vein running down their backs.

Heat the oil in a frying pan, add the ajwain or cumin seeds and the onion and cook until the onion is light golden. Add the turmeric, chilli or paprika and garam masala and cook for 1 minute. Add the chopped peppers, ginger and prawns and sauté over a medium heat for 5–7 minutes, until the prawns are just cooked. Stir in the tomatoes, lemon juice and some salt and cook for 3–4 minutes. Remove from the heat and sprinkle in the chopped coriander.

Make a hole in each poori and fill with the prawn mixture. Place on serving plates, drizzle with the mint, tamarind and yoghurt chutneys and garnish with coriander sprigs.

chinapara's crisp spicy prawns with spring onions

Chinapara means 'Chinese place' – a term for the Chinese community in Kolkata (formerly Calcutta). There has been a Chinese population in India for over three centuries, concentrated mainly around Kolkata. Some of the best Chinese food I have ever eaten came from Tangra in the east of the city. This dish is an enjoyable fusion of Indian and Chinese. The recipe came from Chef Chang, with whom I worked at the Oberoi Hotel in Delhi. He was a great character, with amazing wok skills, and probably more Indian than me during my training days.

SERVES 4

16 medium prawns
2 tablespoons sunflower oil
1 tablespoon chopped garlic
1 dried red chilli, coarsely pounded in
   a pestle and mortar
2 shallots, thinly sliced
1 tablespoon light soy sauce
6 spring onions, thinly sliced
50ml Spicy Indian Ketchup
   (see page 209)
2 slices of canned pineapple, chopped

Peel the prawns and, using the point of a sharp knife, remove the dark, intestinal vein running down their backs.

Heat the oil in a wok, add the garlic and red chilli and sauté for 1 minute. Add the sliced shallots and cook for 1 minute, then add the prawns. Stir-fry over a high heat for 3–5 minutes, until they are almost cooked. Stir in the soy sauce and half the spring onions, sauté for a minute, then add the tomato ketchup and cook for 2–3 minutes. Add the pineapple and heat through. Sprinkle with the remaining spring onions and serve immediately.

prawn FRITTERS WITH fresh tomato-coriander chutney ⟶

JHINGA PAKORAS

This could also be called prawn bhaji. Eating spicy fritters on a rainy day is customary in India. If we did the same in Britain, we would be eating fritters all year round. This versatile recipe can be adapted to virtually anything edible.

SERVES 4

20 medium prawns
vegetable oil for deep-frying
Fresh Tomato and Coriander
  Chutney (see page 208), to serve

For the marinade
1 teaspoon Garlic Paste (see page 202)
½ teaspoon ajwain seeds
1 tablespoon lemon juice
1 teaspoon sunflower oil
sea salt

For the batter
4 tablespoons gram flour
1 tablespoon rice flour
¼ teaspoon red chilli powder
¼ teaspoon dried mango powder
½ tablespoon chopped coriander
  leaves
about 100ml sparkling water

Peel the prawns, leaving the tail section on. With the point of a sharp knife, remove the dark, intestinal vein running down their backs.

Mix all the ingredients for the marinade together. Rub the marinade on to the prawns and leave in the fridge for 15 minutes.

Heat the oil in a deep-fat fryer to 180°C and keep it at this temperature. Mix all the ingredients for the batter together, adding enough sparkling water to give a pouring consistency. Dip the prawns in the batter one by one, holding them by the tail and shaking off the excess batter. Drop them in the hot oil in small batches and fry for 2–3 minutes, until light golden in colour. Transfer to a tray lined with kitchen paper to drain, then serve with the chutney.

malvan prawn fry ⟶

MALVANI JHINGA

Malvan is a small town in Maharashtra, but in cooking terms Malvani refers to the cuisine of the Konkan region of India, which covers parts of Maharashtra, Goa and Karnataka. Its spice combinations are unique, with red chilli leading the flavour every time.

SERVES 4

12–16 medium prawns
2 tablespoons lemon juice
½ teaspoon Malvani Masala
  (see page 204)
¼ teaspoon ground turmeric
½ teaspoon red chilli powder
2 tablespoons Ginger-Garlic Paste
  (see page 202)
4 tablespoons rice flour
4 tablespoons semolina
vegetable oil for frying
sea salt
Spicy Tomato Chutney or Mint and
  Coriander Chutney (see pages 206
  and 207), to serve

Peel the prawns and, using the point of a sharp knife, remove the dark, intestinal vein running down their backs.

Mix the prawns with the lemon juice and a sprinkling of salt and leave to marinate for 15 minutes.

Mix together the Malvani masala, turmeric, chilli and ginger-garlic paste. Apply this paste to the prawns and leave in the fridge for 30–40 minutes.

Mix the rice flour and semolina together on a plate. Pour a 1cm layer of sunflower oil into a large frying pan and place over a medium heat. Dust the prawns in the rice flour and semolina and fry for 2–3 minutes, till golden brown on both sides. Drain on kitchen paper and serve immediately, accompanied by the chutney.

FISH − INDIAN STYLE

thrEE-spicE-crustEd scallops with grapes —

Ever since I first put scallops on my menu, they have been a regular part of my cooking. I have tried ones from all over the UK and even from across the Channel but I find Isle of Man scallops the best. They are quick to cook and have a fantastic natural, juicy sweetness. If you can't get them, use any plump, fresh, diver-caught scallops.

SERVES 4

12 king-sized scallops, coral removed
1½ teaspoons each black and white
  sesame seeds, mixed
½ teaspoon each dried chilli flakes
  and garlic flakes, mixed
½ teaspoon each ground coriander
  and cumin, mixed
3 tablespoons olive or vegetable oil
100g unsalted butter

For the grape sauce
200g mixed black and white seedless
  grapes
50g mint leaves
20g fresh ginger, chopped
¼ small green chilli
1 teaspoon salt
1 teaspoon dried mango powder or
  chaat masala
¼ teaspoon paprika

To garnish
1 young carrot, cut into fine strips
1 punnet of micro salad leaves or pea
  shoots
16 mixed black and white large
  seedless grapes, frozen

To make the grape sauce, mix all the ingredients together, then put them in a blender and blitz until smooth. Set aside.

Dip 4 scallops on one side only in the sesame seeds, Take 4 more scallops and dip one side only in the chilli and garlic flakes. Dip the remaining 4 scallops on one side only in the ground coriander and cumin. Now cook the scallops in 3 separate batches. Heat 1 tablespoon of the oil in a frying pan and add the sesame scallops, sesame-side down. Cook over a medium heat for 30 seconds, then add a third of the butter. Cook for a further ½–1 minute to give a golden colour, then turn and cook for a final minute. Transfer to a warm plate and repeat with the remaining scallops, using fresh oil and butter for each batch.

Divide the carrot strips and micro salad leaves or pea shoots between 4 serving plates and place 3 of each type of scallop on each plate. Drizzle over the grape dressing, place a few frozen grapes beside the scallops and serve immediately.

grilled scallops in the shell with spicy butter —

British scallops are so sweet and beautiful that it would be a crime to process them in any way. This recipe started at Benares as a simple starter with spicy butter, then evolved into something a little more complex. You won't need all the spicy butter here but the leftovers can be used for frying any seafood.

SERVES 4

12 king scallops in the shell, upper
  shell removed (ask your fishmonger
  to do this)
20g unsalted butter, melted
sea salt and freshly ground black
  pepper

For the spicy butter
40g unsalted butter
1 tablespoon chopped coriander
  leaves
1 tablespoon chopped mint
½ teaspoon finely chopped fresh
  ginger
½ teaspoon lime juice
½ teaspoon finely grated lime zest
1 tablespoon unsalted peanuts, lightly
  toasted in a dry frying pan
1 tablespoon finely chopped red
  onion
¼ teaspoon ajwain seeds (or cumin
  seeds), lightly toasted in a dry
  frying pan

To make the spicy butter, put all the ingredients in a food processor, add some salt and pepper and process until well combined. Remove and keep in the fridge until required.

Preheat the grill to high. Brush the scallops with the melted butter and place in a non-stick baking tray, still in their half-shells. Season with salt and pepper. Place under the grill for 1 minute, then remove. Place a teaspoon of the spicy butter on each scallop and return to the grill for 1–2 minutes, until lightly coloured on top. Serve immediately.

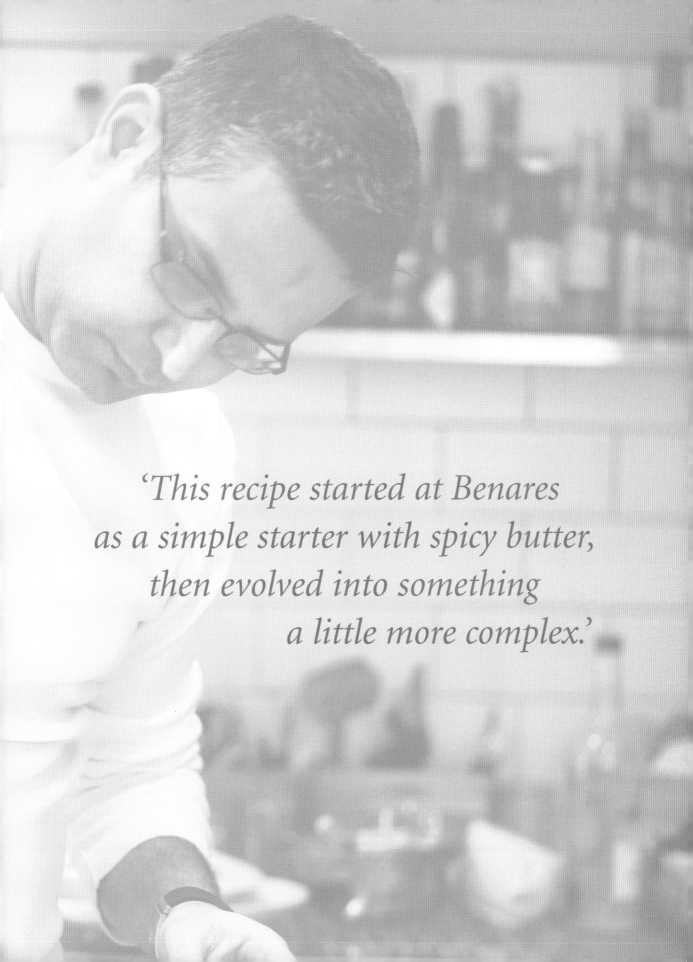

'This recipe started at Benares
as a simple starter with spicy butter,
then evolved into something
a little more complex.'

konkani clams ―

Clams are readily found on both the east and west coasts of India. This superb recipe comes from the Konkan coast on the western side. The spice paste is hot and fragrant, and can be used in curries, roasts and barbecues as well.

Alternative fish
mussels

SERVES 4

600g clams
1 tablespoon lime juice
4 tablespoons sunflower oil
2 onions, chopped
1 tablespoon Ginger-Garlic Paste
  (see page 202)
½ teaspoon ground turmeric
300ml coconut milk
2 tablespoons tamarind pulp
  (see page 218)
2 tablespoons finely chopped
  coriander leaves
sea salt

For the spice paste
5 cloves
8–10 black peppercorns
5cm piece of cinnamon stick
½ teaspoon caraway seeds
2 small dried red chillies
75g desiccated coconut
1 tablespoon sunflower oil
2 onions, thinly sliced and deep-fried
  (see page 202)

First make the spice paste. Put the cloves, peppercorns, cinnamon stick, caraway seeds, chillies and coconut in a heavy-based frying pan and toast over a medium heat, shaking the pan occasionally, until they are aromatic. Leave to cool, then transfer to a food processor or blender with the sunflower oil and onions and blend to a smooth paste.

Wash the clams in cold running water and then drain, discarding any open ones that don't close when tapped on the work surface. Sprinkle the lime juice and some salt over them and set aside for 10–15 minutes.

Heat 2 tablespoons of the oil in a frying pan, add the onions and fry until light golden. Add the ginger-garlic paste and cook for 5 minutes over a medium heat. Add the spice paste and a cup of warm water, then simmer gently for 3–5 minutes.

Heat the remaining oil in a separate pan, add the clams and sauté over a medium heat for 1–2 minutes, until they are just starting to open. Add half a cup of water, cover the pan and cook for 3–4 minutes, till all the clams open. Discard any that remain closed. Add the opened clams to the simmering sauce with the turmeric, coconut milk and tamarind pulp. Cook for 2–3 minutes, then garnish with the coriander and serve at once.

CRAYfiSH saMOSAS —

You can use any kind of seafood to make these samosas but the current abundance of signal crayfish, which were imported to British waters from the USA in the 1970s, has prompted me to feature them more and more in my cooking. They are inexpensive, good quality, and the more of them you eat, the better it will be for our own native English crayfish, whose existence is threatened by these little devils.

Alternative fish
prawns, crab, lobster

SERVES 4

30 live crayfish
2 tablespoons sunflower oil
½ teaspoon mustard seeds
1 tablespoon finely chopped fresh
   ginger
1 small green chilli, finely chopped
2 tablespoons finely chopped onion
5 fresh curry leaves
½ teaspoon ground turmeric
½ teaspoon ground coriander
¼ teaspoon garam masala
1 tablespoon lime juice
1 tablespoon finely chopped
   coriander leaves
12 spring roll wrappers
1 egg, lightly beaten
vegetable oil for deep-frying
sea salt and freshly ground black
   pepper
Spicy Tomato Chutney (see page 206),
   to serve

Put the crayfish in the freezer for an hour or so until almost frozen – this will render them unconscious. Then add them to a very large pan of boiling salted water (do this in batches if necessary, so as not to overcrowd the pan). Bring back to the boil and simmer for 5 minutes, then drain and leave to cool. Peel off the shells and cut the flesh into 1cm dice.

Heat the oil in a frying pan, add the mustard seeds, ginger and green chilli and sauté over a medium heat until the seeds pop. Add the onion and curry leaves and sauté until the onion is translucent. Add the chopped crayfish, sauté for a minute and then stir in the turmeric, coriander and garam masala. Add the lime juice, adjust the seasoning with salt and pepper and then remove from the heat. Sprinkle in the chopped coriander and leave the mixture to cool to room temperature.

Lay the spring roll wrappers out on a work surface. Place 1–2 tablespoons of the filling in a corner of each, fold the wrapper over and then roll into a triangular pastry, brushing the edges with egg to seal. Leave to rest in the fridge for 30 minutes.

Heat the oil to 180°C in a deep-fat fryer or a large, deep saucepan. Add the samosas and fry for about 3 minutes, until light golden and crisp. Drain on kitchen paper and serve straight away, accompanied by the tomato chutney.

chilli-fried potted shrimps ⁓

The best potted shrimps I have ever had were made by my friend, Mark Hix. They tasted divine, and I have had a soft spot for potted shrimps ever since, but sometimes I like them a bit spicier. Here is my version of this great British classic. You can use red or green chilli to infuse the butter with some heat but green works better.

SERVES 4

1 tablespoon olive oil
1 tablespoon finely chopped garlic
1–2 small green chillies, finely chopped (leave the seeds in)
200g unsalted butter
2 tablespoons lime juice
1 small bay leaf
a pinch of freshly grated nutmeg
1 teaspoon anchovy paste
200g peeled brown shrimps
1 tablespoon finely chopped coriander leaves
2 tablespoons finely chopped red onion
sea salt

To serve
brown bread, toasted
2 lemons, halved

Heat the oil in a small pan, add the garlic and green chillies and sauté over a medium heat until the garlic is light brown. Add the butter, reduce the heat and let it melt. Add the lime juice, bay leaf, nutmeg and anchovy paste and simmer for 1 minute. Stir in the shrimps, coriander and onion and remove from the heat. Season well with salt and cool to room temperature. When the butter starts to set, fill 4 ramekins with the mixture.

Remove the ramekins from the fridge at least 15 minutes before serving, so the butter is not too hard to spread on the toast. Serve with the toast and lemon halves.

FISH – INDIAN STYLE

anglo-indian crab cakes

Crab cakes are a common delicacy in Anglo-Indian kitchens. I think it dates back to the days of the Raj, when the English madam, or *memsahib*, needed to prepare an Indian-inspired snack for her soldier husband. This recipe from the *ramu* – a common name for domestic servants – always came in handy.

SERVES 6

2 tablespoons vegetable oil
½ teaspoon cumin seeds
1 small green chilli, finely chopped
1 tablespoon finely chopped garlic
3 tablespoons finely chopped onion
2 tablespoons finely chopped red pepper
2 tablespoons finely chopped green pepper
2 tablespoons desiccated coconut, lightly toasted in a dry frying pan
½ teaspoon red chilli powder
½ teaspoon ground turmeric
300g fresh crab meat (a mixture of brown and white)
100g baked potato flesh, grated
2 tablespoons finely chopped coriander leaves
3 tablespoons plain flour, mixed with 3 tablespoons of water to make a thin batter
2 eggs, lightly beaten
100g fresh breadcrumbs
vegetable oil for deep-frying
Spicy Tomato Chutney or Mint and Coriander Chutney (see pages 206 and 207), to serve

Heat the oil in a frying pan, add the cumin seeds and sauté over a medium heat until they crackle. Add the green chilli and garlic and sauté until the garlic turns light brown. Add the onion and sauté until translucent, then add the chopped peppers. Cook for 3–4 minutes, then stir in the desiccated coconut, chilli powder and turmeric, followed by the crab meat. Cook for 2–3 minutes and then add the grated potato. Mix well, remove from the heat and stir in the chopped coriander. Spread the mixture out on a baking tray and leave to cool. Divide it into 12 pieces and shape them into round patties.

Put the flour and water batter in one bowl, the eggs in another and the breadcrumbs in a third. Dip the patties briefly in the batter, then in the egg and finally in the breadcrumbs. (Dipping the patties in a batter first gives a better finish than dry flour but can make the cakes tricky to handle; if you find they start to break up when you dip them in the batter, you could switch to dry flour instead.) Shape the cakes between your palms to ensure the crumbs adhere well, then leave them to rest in the fridge for 15–20 minutes.

Heat the oil to 180°C in a deep-fat fryer or a large, deep saucepan. Deep-fry the crab cakes, in several batches if necessary, for about 2 minutes, until golden and crisp. Drain on kitchen paper and serve with the chutney.

SOFT-SHELL CRABS WITH *kumquat chutney* ~

KARARA KEKDA

In the UK soft-shell crabs are usually sold frozen. A good fishmonger should be able to order some for you, and they are quite reasonably priced.

SERVES 4

4 jumbo soft-shell crabs
vegetable oil for deep-frying
Kumquat Chutney (see page 209),
   to serve

For the marinade
1 tablespoon Ginger-Garlic Paste
   (see page 202)
½ teaspoon ground turmeric
½ teaspoon ground coriander
¼ teaspoon red chilli powder
1 teaspoon French mustard or
   mustard oil
2 tablespoons chopped coriander leaves
1 tablespoon finely chopped fresh
   ginger
1 tablespoon lime juice
2 tablespoons rice flour
1 tablespoon cornflour
sea salt

Mix all the ingredients for the marinade together and rub them over the crab. Leave to marinate for 30 minutes.

Heat the oil to 180°C in a deep-fat fryer or a large, deep saucepan. Add the crabs and fry for 2–3 minutes, until crisp. Drain on kitchen paper and serve with the chutney.

FISH – INDIAN STYLE

LOBSTER Rillettes

The photo shows this dish presented in a very 'cheffy' way but don't fret about the presentation – it's a great and simple recipe. You could use glass kilner jars, as I have done, or simply put the rillettes in small bowls or even serve on croûtons. It also makes a fabulous sandwich filling – preferably accompanied by a glass of champagne.

Alternative fish
crab, crayfish

SERVES 6–8

2 live lobsters
2 tablespoons vegetable oil
2 sprigs of curry leaves, chopped
2 teaspoons cumin seeds
2 teaspoons mustard seeds
2 tablespoons good-quality
  mayonnaise
1½ tablespoons chopped tarragon
juice of 1 lime, or to taste
sea salt
coriander cress or sprigs of coriander,
  to garnish

First you need to kill the lobsters. Put them in the freezer for 2 hours until almost frozen – this will render them unconscious. Then put each one on a board and plunge a large, sharp knife down through the centre of the head; if you do this confidently, the lobster should die immediately. Add the lobsters to a large pan of boiling water and cook for 1 minute, then remove. Cut off the claws, return them to the pan and cook for another minute or two. Drain well and leave to cool. Remove all the meat from the lobster bodies, discarding the black intestinal vein that runs down the tail flesh and removing the stomach sac and gills from the head. Crack the claws by bashing them with the flat of a large knife and then take out the meat. Cut all the meat into 5mm dice.

Heat the oil in a frying pan, add the curry leaves, cumin seeds and mustard seeds and fry briefly until they crackle. Add the lobster meat and toss for a few minutes, until cooked through. Remove from the heat, leave to cool and then chill thoroughly.

Stir the mayonnaise, chopped tarragon and lime juice into the lobster mixture, then taste and adjust the seasoning. Serve in glass kilner jars or small bowls, garnished with coriander cress or sprigs.

SALADS —

grilled spicy garfish salad with new potatoes

Garfish is commonly called greenbones, too, and its bones are indeed an unusual bright green colour. An agile fish, with fabulous flesh, it comes into shallow waters during spring and summer. This recipe is designed to celebrate summer in the UK.

Alternative fish
mackerel, sardines, any white fish

SERVES 4

12–16 small new potatoes, scrubbed
4 x 300g garfish, filleted
a small bunch of mizuna, rocket or
  mixed salad leaves
a few sprigs of coriander
4 tablespoons vegetable or olive oil
2 tablespoons port or sherry

For the marinade
1 small dried red chilli or 1 teaspoon
  red chilli flakes
¼ teaspoon cumin seeds
¼ teaspoon coriander seeds
¼ teaspoon ajwain seeds
¼ teaspoon ground turmeric
1 teaspoon mustard
½ teaspoon finely chopped fresh
  ginger
1 teaspoon lemon juice
1 tablespoon vegetable oil
sea salt

Cook the potatoes in boiling salted water until tender, then drain and cut in half.

Mix all the ingredients for the marinade together. Brush the fish fillets with the marinade and set aside for 10 minutes.

Toss the salad leaves and coriander sprigs with a tablespoon of the vegetable oil and set aside. Heat the remaining vegetable oil in a ridged cast iron pan (or use a heavy-based frying pan if you don't have a ridged pan), add the garfish fillets and cook over a high heat for about 1 minute on each side, until just done.

Arrange the fish on 4 serving plates with the salad and potatoes. Add any remaining marinade and the port or sherry to the pan in which the fish was cooked, swirl over the heat for 30 seconds and then spoon it over the fish salad. Serve immediately.

FISH – INDIAN STYLE

CRisp fRieD wHitiNG wiTH JerusaLeM ARtiCHOKes, celery aND PEARS in CURRY VINAIgREttE

Whiting is available on UK shores from November to March. Stocks are plentiful and we should eat this fish more often. I love it deep-fried but, to clear my conscience, I serve it with a salad. Jerusalem artichokes are great in autumn and winter but outside these seasons I happily substitute potatoes or carrots.

Alternative fish
pouting, ling, coley, pollack

SERVES 4

400g whiting fillet, skinned
1 tablespoon lemon juice
¼ teaspoon finely grated fresh ginger
vegetable oil for deep-frying
sea salt

For the curry vinaigrette
2 tablespoons cider vinegar or white
  wine vinegar
4 tablespoons olive or sunflower oil
¼ teaspoon curry powder
¼ teaspoon cumin seeds, toasted in a
  dry frying pan and then crushed
¼ teaspoon crushed garlic
1 tablespoon finely chopped red
  onion

For the batter
50g gram flour (or plain flour)
¼ teaspoon ground turmeric
¼ teaspoon ground coriander
½ teaspoon cumin seeds, toasted in a
  dry frying pan
¼ teaspoon red chilli flakes
100ml sparkling water

For the salad
150g Jerusalem artichokes, peeled and sliced
100g celery sticks, cut into thin strips
2 pears, cored and sliced
a small bunch of rocket
a small bunch of bull's blood lettuce or other red lettuce
a little coriander cress, or a few sprigs of coriander

Remove any bones from the whiting and then cut it across the grain into finger-thick strips. Toss them with the lemon juice, ginger and some salt and keep in the fridge until required.

Whisk together all the ingredients for the vinaigrette, season to taste with salt and store in the fridge until required.

Next prepare the Jerusalem artichokes. Blanch them in a pan of boiling salted water for about 3 minutes, until just tender, then drain, refresh in cold water and pat dry. Heat the vegetable oil to 180°C in a deep-fat fryer or a large, deep saucepan and deep-fry the artichoke slices for about 2 minutes, until they are lightly caramelised. Remove and drain on kitchen paper, then keep warm while you cook the fish.

Mix together all the ingredients for the batter. Reheat the vegetable oil to 190°C. Dip the fish in the batter and deep-fry, in batches if necessary, for 2–3 minutes, until crisp and light golden. Drain on kitchen paper and keep warm.

Put the Jerusalem artichokes in a large bowl with all the remaining salad ingredients and toss with about 2 tablespoons of the vinaigrette. Place the fish on top and drizzle over a little more dressing. Serve immediately, with the remaining vinaigrette on the side.

SEARED TROUT WITH ST GEORGE'S MUSHROOMS, RADISHES AND CHEDDAR CHEESE *in* GARLIC AND CHILLI DRESSING

St George's mushrooms may be lesser known than ceps, girolles and morels but they definitely rank amongst the finest wild mushrooms, with a firm texture, appealing flavour and a distinctive aroma reminiscent of soil and wood smoke. In France they are known as 'the true mushroom'. Their appearance in the woods round about St George's Day (April 23rd) is a sign that spring has arrived, as is the reappearance of trout in our rivers – so here's to spring!

Alternative fish
salmon, sea bass, sea bream

SERVES 4

4 trout fillets, cut in half
2 tablespoons gram flour or plain flour
3–4 tablespoons sunflower or olive oil
100g mixed salad leaves (e.g. bull's blood, baby chard, Little Gem)
8–10 radishes, thinly sliced
2 tablespoons finely grated mature Cheddar cheese
sea salt and freshly ground black pepper

For the garlic and chilli dressing
¼ teaspoon finely chopped garlic
1 tablespoon chopped chives or wild garlic leaves
a few strands of saffron
¼ teaspoon red chilli flakes
2 tablespoons olive or sunflower oil
1 tablespoon white wine vinegar

For the mushrooms
1 tablespoon olive or sunflower oil
1 garlic clove, chopped
¼ teaspoon coriander seeds, crushed
¼ teaspoon red chilli flakes
100g St George's mushrooms

Mix together all the ingredients for the dressing and set aside.

Season the trout fillets and dust them with the flour. Heat the oil in a large frying pan, add the fish, skin-side down, and fry over a medium-high heat for 2 minutes, until golden underneath. Turn and cook for 1 minute, then transfer to a warm plate. Cover with foil and keep in a low oven while you cook the mushrooms.

Heat the oil for the mushrooms in a separate pan, add the garlic, coriander seeds and chilli and sauté for a minute over a medium heat. Raise the heat a little and add the mushrooms. Sauté lightly for 3–4 minutes to get a nutty flavour. Season with salt and remove from the heat.

Toss the salad leaves and radishes with half the dressing and divide between 4 plates. Scatter the cheese over, put the mushrooms on top and then the fish. Drizzle the remaining dressing over and serve immediately.

FISH – INDIAN STYLE

SMOKED EEl SAlAD wITH CORiaNDeR-PeaNUT PESTO, ROCKET aND baby ReD cHard

Smoked eel has been a delicacy in the UK since time immemorial. Supplies were sent out to British officers serving in India, where the *memsahibs* used to cook it with great care so as not to waste it. This salad is essentially East Anglian in character but I have 'tempered' it with the liberal use of spices.

There is a huge sustainability issue with eels at the moment. They are now being farmed in the Far East and the Netherlands, so let's hope this helps to bring the eel back to our plates. Till then, please eat with your conscience and enjoy this dish only as an occasional treat.

SERVES 4

150ml soured cream
1 small red onion, finely chopped
¼ teaspoon finely grated lemon zest
¼ teaspoon coriander seeds, toasted
   in a dry frying pan and then crushed
400g smoked eel fillets
a handful of rocket
a handful of baby red chard leaves
2 hard-boiled eggs, peeled and cut
   into quarters

For the coriander-peanut pesto
6 tablespoons plain unsalted peanuts
   (or pine nuts), lightly toasted in a
   dry frying pan
50g coriander leaves
2 garlic cloves, chopped
a pinch of red chilli flakes
6 tablespoons olive oil
2 tablespoons lemon juice
sea salt

Put all the ingredients for the pesto in a food processor and blend to a fine paste, adding a little warm water if necessary. Mix the pesto with the soured cream, then stir in the red onion, lemon zest and toasted coriander seeds to make a dressing.

Snip the eel fillets into smaller pieces and mix with the rocket and baby chard. Divide the salad between 4 serving plates, place the eggs on each plate, then drizzle with the dressing and serve.

PURpLe sprouting BROCCOLI aND salmon salaD with poaching LIQUID Dressing ~

As a chef, I have to say that wild salmon is the best but the truth is I try not to use it. At my restaurants I now use organic farmed salmon, which is very nearly as good. We caterers have to take some responsibility for the over fishing of this species.

I have made this recipe many times in my own home. It's popular with kids but if they don't like it too spicy, just omit the chilli.

Alternative fish ~
sea trout, brown and rainbow trout, even grayling – or you could use a white fish such as dab, flounder or lemon sole

SERVES 4

600ml Fish Stock (see page 203)
2 tablespoons coriander (or parsley) stalks, chopped
1 tablespoon finely chopped fresh ginger
1 teaspoon finely chopped green chilli
1 teaspoon cumin seeds, toasted in a dry frying pan and then ground to a powder
1 teaspoon sesame seeds, toasted in a dry frying pan
200g purple sprouting broccoli
400g salmon fillet, cut into 8 pieces
200g mixed colourful salad leaves (e.g. bull's blood, baby chard, Little Gem, etc.)

For the dressing
2 tablespoons sunflower oil
1 garlic clove, finely chopped
1 tablespoon finely chopped onion

¼ teaspoon ground turmeric
1 teaspoon finely chopped fresh ginger
½ teaspoon finely chopped red chilli
½ teaspoon sesame seeds, toasted in a dry frying pan
½ teaspoon cumin seeds, toasted in a dry frying pan and then crushed
½ tablespoon finely chopped coriander leaves
2 tablespoons lemon juice
sea salt

Bring the fish stock to a simmer in a pan and add the coriander stalks, ginger, green chilli, ground cumin and sesame seeds. Blanch the broccoli in the stock for 5 minutes, until just tender, then remove with a slotted spoon and refresh immediately in cold water to stop it cooking further. Drain well and set aside.

Add the salmon pieces to the simmering stock and poach for 3–4 minutes. Remove from the liquid with a slotted spoon and set aside. Reserve the poaching liquid.

To make the dressing, heat the oil in a pan, add the garlic and onion and sauté lightly until translucent. Add the turmeric, ginger, red chilli, sesame seeds, crushed cumin, coriander leaves and some salt and sauté for 1 minute. Stir in the lemon juice and 100ml of the warm poaching liquid. Remove from the heat and let it cool to room temperature.

Divide the broccoli, salad leaves and salmon between 4 deep plates. Pour the poaching liquid dressing over and serve.

'I have made this recipe many times in my own home. It's popular with kids but if they don't like it too spicy, just omit the chilli.'

LOBSTER AND AVOCADO SALAD ⟶

Lobster and avocado is a great combination. I love using mayonnaise in salads but adding mango chutney and lime zest gives it a new dimension entirely. The combination of lime and mango reminds me of childhood summers in India.

Alternative fish
crab, crayfish, prawns

SERVES 4

2 live lobsters, weighing about 800g each
2 large avocados, peeled, stoned and sliced
1 large orange, peeled and divided into segments
a small bunch of mizuna or baby rocket (or other lettuce leaves)
1 tablespoon olive oil
½ tablespoon lime juice

For the dressing
6–8 tablespoons mayonnaise
2 tablespoons sweet mango chutney
1 teaspoon finely grated lime zest
1 tablespoon lime juice
1 red onion, finely chopped
1 tablespoon finely chopped coriander leaves
1 green chilli, finely chopped
2 teaspoons finely chopped fresh ginger

Put the lobsters in the freezer for 2 hours until almost frozen – this will render them unconscious. Meanwhile, mix together all the ingredients for the dressing and keep in the fridge until needed.

Put the semi-frozen lobsters in a very large pan of boiling salted water, bring back to the boil and simmer for 15 minutes. Drain, refresh in chilled water and then cut each one in half from head to tail. Remove the tail meat, discarding the black intestinal vein that runs down the centre. Crack open the claws by bashing them with the flat of a large knife and then take out the meat, keeping it as intact as possible. Cut the tail meat into dice but leave the claw meat whole. Mix the lobster meat with the sliced avocado, orange segments and salad leaves, drizzle with the olive oil and lime juice, then divide between 4 serving plates. Serve the dressing on the side.

CRAB CLAWS WITH GRILLED ASPARAGUS IN SEA LAVENDER HONEY AND CORIANDER DRESSING

Sea lavender honey is a Norfolk speciality but if you can't get it, don't worry. Just use ordinary honey or lavender honey and the results will still be very good. Cromer crab, local asparagus and local honey – this is what makes this recipe so appealing, but I have tweaked it with spices to make it even better. I prefer grilling the asparagus to blanching it. All the nutrients are preserved in this way and you also get the flavour of the chargrill.

You can buy crab claws frozen and the quality is very good – ask at your local fishmongers if they can order some for you. If using fresh crab claws, you will have to blanch them for 5 minutes and then remove the shells.

SERVES 4

16 large crab claws
sunflower oil for deep-frying
20 asparagus spears, peeled to about
    half way up the stem
100g mixed salad leaves
8 baby plum tomatoes, cut in half

For the marinade
1 tablespoon Garlic Paste (see page 202)
½ teaspoon red chilli powder
¼ teaspoon ground turmeric
¼ teaspoon ajwain seeds, toasted in a
    dry frying pan
¼ teaspoon dried mango powder
1 tablespoon lemon juice

For the dressing
3 tablespoons sunflower or olive oil
1 tablespoon finely chopped fresh ginger
1 tablespoon finely chopped coriander roots
1 teaspoon coriander seeds, lightly crushed
½ teaspoon finely chopped green chilli
2 tablespoons sea lavender honey
1 tablespoon lemon juice
1 tomato, skinned, deseeded and diced
1 tablespoon finely chopped coriander leaves
4 tablespoons Fish Stock (see page 203)
½ teaspoon finely grated lemon zest
sea salt and freshly ground black pepper

For the batter
200g plain flour
a pinch of sea salt
250ml beer

Mix together all the ingredients for the marinade, rub them over the crab claws and set aside for 5 minutes.

For the dressing, heat the oil in a small pan, add the ginger, coriander roots, coriander seeds and chilli and sauté for a minute, until they sizzle. Remove from the heat, add the rest of the ingredients and mix well. Set aside.

To make the batter, sift the flour and salt into a bowl and gradually whisk in the beer. Heat the sunflower oil to 180–190°C in a deep-fat fryer or a large, deep saucepan. Dip the crab claws in the batter one by one and add them to the hot oil. Fry for about 2 minutes, until light golden and crisp, then transfer to kitchen paper to soak up excess oil. Keep warm while you cook the asparagus.

Toss the asparagus in a tablespoon of sunflower oil and cook on a ridged grill pan for 4–5 minutes, until tender and lightly charred, turning regularly. Cut into 5cm batons. Divide the salad leaves, tomatoes and asparagus between 4 plates and place 4 crab claws on each. Drizzle a little of the dressing over the salad and serve the rest on the side.

CRAB salaD WITH CORiaNDeR aND CURRY Leaves —

Crabs are available on British shores throughout the year but are at their best in the summer. In India, you usually find sea crabs, which are like the British brown crab, and mud crabs, similar to blue velvet swimmer crabs – both suitable for this recipe. Here in the UK, I would use brown, blue velvet swimmer or spider crabs. I do think that blue velvet swimmers are very underrated, and they can be excellent in stews and curries.

In India and Thailand, this salad is served on a betel leaf, which you roll up and eat with your fingers.

Alternative fish
lobster

SERVES 4

1½ tablespoons vegetable or coconut
   oil
½ teaspoon mustard seeds
10 curry leaves, chopped
1 teaspoon finely chopped fresh ginger
½ teaspoon finely chopped green chilli
1 onion, chopped
300g fresh white crab meat
1 teaspoon ground turmeric
¾ teaspoon salt
3 tablespoons coconut milk
1 teaspoon chopped coriander leaves
1 tablespoon grated fresh coconut (or
   desiccated coconut)

To serve
Passion Fruit and Sweet Chilli Sauce
   (see page 208) or Kumquat Chutney
   (see page 209)
a handful of baby salad leaves

Heat the oil in a frying pan and add the mustard seeds. When they start to splutter, add the curry leaves and sauté for 30 seconds. Then add the ginger and green chilli and cook for another 30 seconds. Add the onion and sauté until translucent. Add the crab meat, sauté for 2–3 minutes, then stir in the turmeric and salt. Sauté for 2 minutes over a medium heat and then add the coconut milk, coriander leaves and grated coconut. Remove from the heat and leave to cool. Serve accompanied by a chutney and the salad leaves.

FISH – INDIAN STYLE

CRAYFISH SALAD WITH WILD GARLIC DRESSING —

While cooking with Mark Hix and James Martin on various television shows, I learned a lot about signal crayfish, its origins and its predatory nature, from which our own native crayfish have suffered. I use crayfish a lot on my menus throughout the year, and its abundance should prompt every British cook to do so.

Alternative fish
prawns

SERVES 4

2 tablespoons sunflower or olive oil
50g butter
24 live crayfish
2 carrots, thinly sliced
1 small red onion, thinly sliced
1 tablespoon finely chopped fresh
  ginger
1 tablespoon chopped mint
¼ teaspoon ground turmeric
¼ teaspoon ground coriander
a pinch of garam masala
50ml Fish Stock (see page 203)
a small bunch of rocket
sea salt

For the dressing
2 tablespoons chopped wild garlic
  leaves
1 tablespoon chopped coriander
  leaves
1 teaspoon cumin seeds, toasted in a
  dry frying pan and then crushed
100ml soured cream
1 teaspoon finely grated lemon zest
1 tablespoon lemon juice
a pinch of freshly grated nutmeg

Put the crayfish in the freezer for an hour or so until almost frozen – this will render them unconscious. Heat the oil and butter in a large pan, add the crayfish and sauté over a medium heat for 4–6 minutes, until pink. Remove from the pan and then strain the oil through a fine sieve. As soon as the crayfish are cool enough to handle, remove the shells and de-vein them by picking out the dark intestinal vein running down the back of each one with the tip of a sharp knife. Set aside.

For the dressing, mix all the ingredients together, season with salt and then set aside.

Tip the strained oil and butter back into the pan in which you cooked the crayfish. Add the carrots, red onion, ginger and mint and sauté lightly for 2–3 minutes, until softened. Stir in the turmeric, coriander, garam masala and a little salt, then add the crayfish and sauté for 1–2 minutes, until they are thoroughly reheated and lightly coated with the spices. Add the fish stock, simmer gently for 2–3 minutes, then remove from the heat.

Divide the rocket leaves between 4 plates and put the crayfish and carrot mixture on top. Serve with a dollop of the soured cream dressing.

fish for everyday ⁓

a simple fish curry ~

Fish curries are extremely common in coastal India. Each region has its own version with its characteristic spicing. I have chosen simple spices here to make an everyday dish, and cooked the fish separately from the sauce to give it a better flavour and texture.

Alternative fish
pollack, whiting, pouting

SERVES 4

4 tablespoons sunflower oil
1 teaspoon cumin seeds
1 onion, sliced
½ teaspoon ground turmeric
½ teaspoon ground coriander
¼ teaspoon red chilli powder
200ml Fish Stock (see page 203) or
   water
2 small tomatoes, thickly sliced
½ tablespoon lemon juice
4 pieces of farmed cod fillet, weighing
   about 125g each
a pinch of garam masala
2 tablespoons finely chopped
   coriander leaves
sea salt and freshly ground black
   pepper

Heat half the oil in a saucepan, add the cumin seeds and sauté over a medium heat until they start to pop. Add the onion and sauté until translucent. Stir in the turmeric, coriander and chilli powder. Sauté for 1 minute, pour in the stock or water and bring to a simmer. Add the tomato slices and lemon juice and cook over a low heat for 3–5 minutes, until the tomatoes have softened. Adjust the seasoning, if necessary.

Brush the fish with the remaining oil and season with salt and pepper. Cook, skin-side up, under a hot grill for 4–5 minutes, until the skin is crisp, then turn and cook the other side for 3–4 minutes, depending on the thickness of the fish.

Put the fish on 4 serving plates and pour the sauce over. Sprinkle with the garam masala and coriander and serve with boiled rice.

GrIlleD TurBoT MaRInaTeD in MANgo PickLe paste with CUCUMBER-MoOli SAlAD

ACHARI MACHCHI

Cooking fish with pickles or traditional pickle flavours is an old practice. This recipe is very simple and works well on the grill, barbecue or in the oven.

Mooli is a long, white radish, also known as daikon. You should be able to find it in Asian shops and some supermarkets.

Alternative fish
haddock, halibut, John Dory

SERVES 4

4 x 100g pieces of turbot fillet
30g butter, melted
Mint and Coriander Chutney
   (see page 207), to serve

For the marinade
1 teaspoon Garlic Paste (see page 202)
2 tablespoons Mango Pickle Paste
   (see page 202)
1 teaspoon fennel seeds, toasted in a
   dry frying pan and then ground to
   a powder
1 tablespoon mustard oil or vegetable
   oil
1 teaspoon finely chopped fresh ginger

For the cucumber-mooli salad
1 tablespoon vegetable or sunflower
   oil
½ teaspoon mustard seeds
1 dried red chilli
3–5 curry leaves
1 tablespoon white wine vinegar
½ teaspoon sugar
1 small cucumber, halved lengthways
   and sliced

1 small mooli, halved lengthways
   and sliced
a small bunch of rocket
sea salt

Mix together all the ingredients for the marinade and rub them over the fish. Leave in the fridge to marinate for 30 minutes.

Place the fish on a baking tray and sear under a very hot grill for about 1½ minutes per side, until coloured. Brush with some of the melted butter and transfer to an oven preheated to 180°C/Gas Mark 4 for 5–7 minutes to complete the cooking. Remove from the oven, baste with more butter and keep warm.

Meanwhile, for the salad, heat the oil in a small frying pan and add the mustard seeds, red chilli and curry leaves. When the mustard seeds start to pop, remove from the heat and stir in the white wine vinegar, sugar and some salt, then return to a medium heat for a minute. Remove from the heat again and stir in the cucumber and mooli.

Mix the rocket leaves with the warm mooli and cucumber and divide between 4 plates. Place the fish on top and serve with the mint chutney.

perch with spicy tomato sauce ~

MACHCHI KADHAI

Kadhai cooking originates from northern India and relies on a few principal ingredients – mainly coriander seeds, garlic and red chilli – for its distinctive character.

Alternative fish
any firm white fish

SERVES 4

4 large perch fillets
1 tablespoon sunflower oil
1 tablespoon butter
1 small green pepper, cut into thin strips
1 small yellow pepper, cut into thin strips
1 small red onion, thinly sliced
coriander cress or sprigs of coriander, to garnish
sea salt and freshly ground black pepper

For the spicy tomato sauce
1½ tablespoons sunflower oil
1½ teaspoons finely chopped garlic
1 teaspoon coriander seeds, crushed
½ teaspoon red chilli flakes
400g tomatoes, skinned, deseeded and chopped
1 teaspoon ground coriander
¼ teaspoon garam masala
½ teaspoon powdered dried fenugreek leaves
1 teaspoon lemon juice

First make the sauce. Heat the oil in a pan and add the garlic, coriander seeds and red chilli flakes. As the garlic starts to turn light golden, add the tomatoes. Cook gently until they turn into a pulp, then add the ground coriander, garam masala and fenugreek. Stir in the lemon juice and some salt to taste.

Season the fish fillets with salt and pepper. Heat the oil in a large frying pan, add the fish, skin-side down, and fry over a medium heat for about 2 minutes per side, until just cooked through. Add the butter to the pan and use to baste the fish, then remove the fish from the pan and keep warm. Add the peppers and onion to the pan and sauté for 1–2 minutes, until slightly softened. Pour in the sauce and toss well. Divide between 4 plates, place the fish on top, then garnish with the coriander. Serve with rice or bread.

south indian vermicelli with squid —

MAKALI UPMA

This is a fantastic recipe from southern India. Although I have used squid here, it can be made with any fish, or even with vegetables. The spicing is simple and straightforward.

SERVES 4

500g vermicelli
2 tablespoons vegetable oil
2 cloves
3cm piece of cinnamon stick
2 cardamom pods
1 onion, chopped
2 green chillies, chopped
1 tomato, chopped
1 teaspoon Ginger-Garlic Paste (see page 202)
600ml hot water
1 tablespoon chopped coriander leaves
sea salt

For the squid
200g cleaned baby squid, cut into rings
½ teaspoon red chilli powder
1 teaspoon ground coriander
½ teaspoon ground turmeric
1 tablespoon lemon juice
3 tablespoons rice flour
vegetable oil for deep-frying

For the squid, mix all the ingredients except the oil together, season with salt and set aside.

Heat a wok, add the vermicelli and fry, without any oil, for 3–4 minutes, until it colours lightly; do not let it brown. Remove from the wok and set aside.

Heat the oil in the wok, add the cloves, cinnamon and cardamom and sauté over a medium heat until they pop. Add the onion and green chillies and fry until the onion is brown. Add the tomato and the ginger-garlic paste and fry for 3–4 minutes, until the tomato is soft. Pour in the hot water, season with salt and bring to the boil. Add the vermicelli and stir for 3–5 minutes, until all the water has been absorbed. Remove from the heat and keep warm.

To cook the squid, heat the oil to 190°C in a deep-fat fryer or a deep saucepan and fry the squid rings until light golden and crisp. Drain on kitchen paper and serve with the vermicelli, garnished with the chopped coriander.

FISH – INDIAN STYLE

*fi*SH MASALA *WITH* AJWAIN PARA*thas*

In India, I use seer, which is a member of the mackerel family, or kingfish for this recipe but in the UK there is so much variety that you could use almost anything. A firm, meaty fish, such as turbot, swordfish or grouper, would work particularly well.

SERVES 4

500g fish fillets, skinned and cut into
  2.5cm cubes
1 tablespoon gram flour
vegetable oil for deep-frying
4 Ajwain Parathas (see page 214)
sea salt

For the marinade
1 tablespoon Ginger-Garlic Paste
  (see page 202)
1 tablespoon lemon juice
1 teaspoon ground turmeric
½ teaspoon red chilli powder
¼ teaspoon garam masala

For the masala
2 tablespoons vegetable oil
1 teaspoon cumin seeds
½ teaspoon red chilli flakes
1 teaspoon crushed garlic
1 large onion, thinly sliced
4 tomatoes, chopped
1 teaspoon ground coriander
1 teaspoon ground turmeric
½ teaspoon garam masala
½ teaspoon powdered dried
  fenugreek leaves
2 tablespoons finely chopped
  coriander leaves

Mix all the marinade ingredients together, season with salt, then stir in the cubes of fish. Set aside to marinate for 20–30 minutes.

For the masala, heat the oil in a pan, add the cumin seeds, red chilli flakes and garlic and sauté for 1–2 minutes, until the garlic colours lightly. Add the onion and sauté for 10–12 minutes, until lightly browned. Add the tomatoes and sauté for 10 minutes, until softened and collapsed. Stir in all the ground spices, cook for 3–5 minutes and then remove from the heat. Season with salt and stir in the chopped coriander.

Dust the fish with the gram flour. Heat the vegetable oil to 180°C in a deep-fat fryer or a deep saucepan. Add the fish and fry until sealed and lightly coloured all over, then drain on kitchen paper. Mix the fried fish into the masala sauce and serve immediately, with the ajwain parathas.

kedgeree —

Kichri, or kedgeree, is an easy everyday meal. Indians use lentils and the British use fish in their recipes. Both are legitimate, but for me this British-Indian version works best of all – it includes both.

Alternative fish
any white fish

SERVES 4

400g pollack or ling fillet, cut into
   8 slices
1 tablespoon butter or ghee
2½ tablespoons vegetable oil
3 cloves
3cm piece of cinnamon stick
1 bay leaf
1 teaspoon cumin seeds
20g piece of fresh ginger, finely chopped
1 small dried red chilli
200g long grain white rice
60g yellow split peas
30g mung lentils
70g fresh coconut, grated (see page 216),
   or desiccated coconut
½ teaspoon ground turmeric
400ml Fish Stock (see page 203) or
   warm water
1½ teaspoons salt
a pinch of sugar
1 tablespoon chopped coriander
   leaves
Coriander and Peanut Chutney
   (see page 207), to serve

For the marinade
¼ teaspoon salt
½ tablespoon lemon juice
½ teaspoon red chilli powder
½ teaspoon ground turmeric

Mix together all the ingredients for the marinade and rub them over the fish. Leave to marinate for 30 minutes.

Heat the butter or ghee and a tablespoon of the oil in a large saucepan, add the cloves, cinnamon stick, bay leaf, cumin seeds, ginger and red chilli and cook for about a minute, until they splutter. Add the rice, yellow split peas, mung lentils and coconut and sauté for a minute or two. Add the turmeric, fish stock or water, salt and sugar and cook over a low heat for 10–15 minutes, until the rice and lentils are tender. Remove from the heat, sprinkle with the chopped coriander and keep warm.

Heat the remaining oil in a frying pan and fry the pieces of fish over a medium heat for 1–2 minutes per side. Divide the kedgeree between 4 serving bowls, put the fish on top and then top with the coriander and peanut chutney.

iNDiaN-STyle seafood LiNguine ~

I love the flavour of the garlic and curry leaves in this dish. Rice noodles are used a lot in southern India, and especially in Kerala, where this recipe originates. In Kerala, people would make their own noodles using a press. Here in the UK, several different types of rice noodles are available and you can use what you like – even flat rice noodles can produce a very decent result.

SERVES 4

2 tablespoons sunflower oil
3 garlic cloves, chopped
½ teaspoon mustard seeds
1 small green chilli, chopped
1 small onion, chopped
10 curry leaves, roughly chopped
½ teaspoon ground turmeric
¼ teaspoon red chilli flakes, plus extra to garnish
¼ teaspoon ground coriander
600g ripe tomatoes, deseeded and chopped
500g rice noodles (or wheat noodles, such as linguine)
a pinch of garam masala
1 tablespoon finely chopped coriander leaves
sea salt

1kg prepared mixed shellfish – choose from: langoustines; small, unpeeled raw prawns; clams, mussels, cockles, razor clams, cooked; white crab meat

Heat the oil in a large pan, add the garlic, mustard seeds and green chilli and sauté until the seeds begin to pop. Add the onion, sauté for a few minutes, until translucent, then add the curry leaves and cook for 2 minutes. Add the turmeric, chilli flakes and ground coriander, sauté for 1 minute, then stir in the tomatoes. Cook slowly for 8–10 minutes, until soft and pulpy. Meanwhile, cook the noodles in a large pan of boiling salted water until *al dente*.

Add the langoustines to the sauce and cook for 2 minutes, until they turn pink. Add the prawns and simmer for 2–3 minutes, until cooked. Stir in the cooked shellfish and crab meat and heat through well. Correct the seasoning with salt and sprinkle with the garam masala, coriander leaves and a few red chilli flakes. Drain the pasta, toss with the sauce and serve immediately.

sea bass with a green spice crust

KHOJA FISH MASALA

The Khoja community in India are an offshoot of an Islamic Shia sect. They are excellent cooks and their food has a real 'wow' factor. I have given this simple recipe a little twist by grilling the fish.

SERVES 4

Alternative fish
mackerel, sardines, red snapper, grey
  mullet

4 sea bass fillets

For the green spice crust
2 tablespoons vegetable oil
6 curry leaves, chopped
½ teaspoon mustard seeds
200g fresh coconut, grated (see page 216),
  then whizzed to a rough paste in a
  food processor with 4 tablespoons
  coconut milk
½ teaspoon crushed black
  peppercorns
2 tablespoons coriander leaves, whizzed
  to a paste in a food processor
  with 1 tablespoon tamarind pulp
  (see page 218)
½ teaspoon ground turmeric
4–6 tablespoons coconut milk
2 tablespoons crushed pine nuts
sea salt

First prepare the spice crust. Heat the oil in a pan, add the curry leaves and mustard seeds and sauté over a medium heat until the seeds crackle. Add the coconut paste and crushed peppercorns and sauté for about 2 minutes, until the coconut is pale golden. Stir in the coriander and tamarind paste, plus the turmeric and enough coconut milk to bind. Season with salt, remove from the heat and stir in the crushed pine nuts. Leave to cool.

Apply this paste liberally to the flesh side of the sea bass fillets and then place them on a greased baking sheet. Place in an oven preheated to 180°C/Gas Mark 6 and bake for 6–8 minutes, until cooked through. Serve hot, accompanied by a green leafy salad or a cucumber and tomato salad.

paella-style fish biryani —

This is a very rustic version of biryani. You could add lobster, mussels or whatever seafood you like – just use your imagination to make this dish special. The seafood is cooked in the biryani, but to enhance the flavour I sometimes fry it separately and add it at the end.

SERVES 4

150g red snapper fillet
150g sea bream fillet
12 cooked tiger prawns
2 tablespoons sunflower oil
1 tablespoon butter or ghee
1 clove
1 bay leaf
1 small onion, sliced
1 green chilli, chopped
300g white long grain or basmati rice
600ml Fish Stock (see page 203)
2 tablespoons finely chopped
   coriander leaves
1 lime, cut into wedges, to garnish

For the sauce
1 tablespoon sunflower oil
½ teaspoon cumin seeds
1 garlic clove, chopped
1 teaspoon finely chopped fresh
   ginger
1 onion, chopped
2 tomatoes, chopped
1 red pepper, chopped
½ teaspoon red chilli powder
½ teaspoon ground turmeric
1 teaspoon ground coriander
½ teaspoon garam masala
1 tablespoon lemon juice
sea salt

To make the sauce, heat the oil in a pan, add the cumin seeds and sauté over a medium heat until they pop. Add the garlic and ginger, then as the garlic changes colour, stir in the onion. Sauté until lightly coloured. Add the tomatoes and red pepper and sauté until the tomatoes are soft. Stir in the chilli powder, turmeric, coriander and garam masala and sauté for 2 minutes. Add the lemon juice and some salt to taste and cook for 3–4 minutes. Remove from the heat and blend the mixture to a smooth paste in a blender or food processor.

Cut the snapper and bream fillets into small pieces. Peel the prawns and, using the point of a sharp knife, remove the dark, intestinal vein running down their backs. Set aside.

Heat the oil and butter or ghee in a large, heavy-based saucepan and add the clove, bay leaf, onion and chilli. Sauté until the onion is translucent, then add the rice and sauté for 2 minutes. Add the blended sauce and half the fish stock and simmer, uncovered, until the liquid has almost all been absorbed by the rice. Add the fish and prawns, pour in the remaining stock and cook for 7–10 minutes, until the liquid has been absorbed and the rice is tender. Sprinkle with the chopped coriander, garnish with lime wedges and serve.

*fi*SH KEBAB AND C*h*ips *i*N a ro*ll* —

Kebab rolls are street snacks from northern India, which can be filled with anything from vegetables to meat. Fish kebab rolls are no novelty but here I have given them a little British twist.

SERVES 4

1 quantity of cooked Salmon Brochettes Marinated in Mustard and Honey (see page 35)
150g well-fried chips (oven-ready chips are fine)
2 tablespoons mayonnaise
1 tablespoon mango chutney, chopped
1 tablespoon chopped mint
100g mixed salad leaves
½ teaspoon cumin seeds, lightly toasted in a dry frying pan and then crushed
½ teaspoon finely chopped green chilli
4 tortillas or ready-made chapattis
Mint and Coriander Chutney (see page 207) or Spicy Indian Ketchup (see page 209), to serve

Put the hot salmon in a bowl and add the chips, mayonnaise, chutney, mint, salad leaves, toasted cumin and green chilli.

Lightly heat each tortilla or chapatti in a dry frying pan. Place them on a work surface, divide the filling between them and then fold in the sides and roll up. Cut in half and serve with mint chutney or ketchup.

sea bream pasties with gooseberry chutney —

GUJIA

Gujia is a festive food in India, made as a sweet during Holi, the festival of colours. There is a lesser-known savoury variety called *ghungra*, which is also the name of a Rajasthani dance. I like to make the savoury variety with fresh peas during the summer months but this fish version is also exquisite. If you don't want to make your own pastry, bought puff pastry does a decent job.

Alternative fish
sea bass, trout, turbot, John Dory

SERVES 4

2 tablespoons sunflower oil
1 teaspoon ajwain seeds
1 teaspoon finely chopped garlic
1 onion, thinly sliced
½ teaspoon red chilli flakes
½ teaspoon ground coriander
½ teaspoon ground turmeric
¼ teaspoon garam masala
1 teaspoon finely chopped fresh
   ginger
100ml double cream or coconut milk
300g sea bream fillets, skinned and
   cut into 2.5cm cubes
1 tablespoon finely chopped
   coriander leaves
sea salt
Gooseberry Chutney (see page 206),
   to serve

For the pastry
200g plain flour
½ teaspoon ajwain seeds or cumin
   seeds, toasted in a dry frying pan
100g unsalted butter, diced
3–4 tablespoons cold water

1 egg, beaten with a pinch of sugar
   and a tablespoon of milk, for
   glazing

First make the pastry. Put the flour and seeds in a bowl, then rub in the butter with your fingertips until the mixture resembles fine breadcrumbs. Gradually stir in enough water to bring the mixture together into a dough. Knead lightly and then cover with a damp cloth and leave to rest in the fridge while you prepare the filling.

Heat the oil in a frying pan, add the ajwain seeds and garlic and sauté until the garlic changes colour. Add the sliced onion and chilli flakes and sauté for 2–3 minutes, until the onion is translucent. Stir in the ground coriander, turmeric and garam masala and sauté for 1 minute. Add the ginger and double cream or coconut milk, bring to a simmer and remove from the heat. Stir in the fish cubes and chopped coriander and season to taste.

Cut the pastry into quarters and roll out each piece into a circle 18–20cm in diameter. Divide the filling between the circles, putting it in the centre of each one. Brush the edges of the pastry with the egg mixture and then bring the pastry up over the filling (like Cornish pasties). Crimp the edges together to seal them, using your fingers or a fork.

Place the pasties on a baking sheet and brush them with the remaining egg glaze. Bake in an oven preheated to 200°C/Gas Mark 6 for 30–35 minutes, until golden brown. Eat hot or cold, with the gooseberry chutney.

beŋgalɪ-styłe frɪeđ fɪsh ~

MACHER BHAJA

This dish brings back memories of my childhood in East India. On cold winter evenings, as housewives stoked their charcoal-fired stoves outside their houses to get the fuel burning properly before moving them into the kitchen, a fish vendor used to appear dramatically out of the smoke. His fried fish was so simple, yet so full of flavour, and the aroma of his spice mixes use to get me salivating.

SERVES 4

4 medium-sized round fish steaks,
  such as salmon, kingfish or sea bass
vegetable oil for frying

For the marinade
1 teaspoon red chilli powder
1 teaspoon ground coriander
½ teaspoon ground turmeric
1 teaspoon dried mango powder
1 tablespoon lemon juice
½ tablespoon mustard oil or
  vegetable oil
1 teaspoon finely chopped fresh
  ginger
½ tablespoon gram flour
sea salt

For the salad
1 small cucumber, diced
1 tomato, diced
½ tablespoon chopped coriander
  leaves
1 teaspoon lemon juice
a pinch of sugar
¼ teaspoon cumin seeds, lightly
  toasted in a dry frying pan and then
  coarsely crushed
sea salt

Mix together all the ingredients for the marinade, adding the gram flour last. Smear the paste over the fish and set aside for 10–15 minutes.

Heat a 1.5cm-deep layer of oil in a deep frying pan - the oil should come half way up the sides of the fish. Add the fish and cook over a medium heat for 2–3 minutes on each side, then remove from the pan and drain on kitchen paper. If the fish is still raw in the centre, finish the cooking in a hot oven for a couple of minutes.

Toss together all the ingredients for the salad and serve immediately with the fish.

FISH – INDIAN STYLE

goa's mackerel recheado with green apple and star fruit salad ~

Recheado means stuffed, and traditionally the fish are stuffed with a very hot, pungent spice paste. I have toned it down a little but if you still find it too hot, serve a dish of yoghurt with the mackerel.

Alternative fish
sardines, mullet

SERVES 4

4 mackerel, filleted, pin bones removed
vegetable oil for shallow-frying

For the spice paste
2 dried red chillies
3 cloves
10 large garlic cloves
1 teaspoon cumin seeds
1 teaspoon coriander seeds
1 teaspoon fennel seeds
8 black peppercorns
1 cinnamon stick
6 green cardamom pods
2 teaspoons ground turmeric
6 Dutch red chillies
1 teaspoon brown sugar or palm sugar
4 tablespoons Tamarind Pulp (see page 218)
red wine vinegar

For the salad
2 star fruit, diced
2 green apples, cored and diced
1 celery stick, thinly sliced
1 carrot, thinly sliced
1 teaspoon lime juice

½ teaspoon cumin seeds, lightly toasted in a dry frying pan and then crushed
1 tablespoon olive oil
1 teaspoon chopped mint

Blend all the ingredients for the spice paste together in a food processor, adding enough vinegar to make a thick paste. Place a mackerel fillet on a board, skin-side down, and spread a layer of paste on it. Place another fillet on top with the skin side up to make a sandwich. Tie in 2 or 3 places with string, so the spice paste doesn't pop out during cooking. Repeat with the remaining fillets and spice paste.

Heat a thin layer of oil in a large frying pan, add the mackerel and fry for about 2–3 minutes on each side, until just cooked through.

Mix all the ingredients for the salad together and toss well. Serve with the fish.

konkani fish curry in a spicy coconut sauce ⟿

AALLE KAANDYA AAMBAT

An amazing variety of fish is landed on the Konkan coast. Konkan people consume spicy food like nowhere else in India. In this simple recipe I like to cook the fish separately from the sauce in order to preserve its texture. However, if you prefer to cook the fish in the sauce, please do so – after all, that's the tradition!

Alternative fish
mackerel, pomfret, kingfish, sardines

SERVES 4

250g fresh coconut, grated (see page 216)
200ml Fish Stock (see page 203) or
  water
1–2 dried red chillies, to taste
1 teaspoon coriander seeds
2 tablespoons Tamarind Pulp
  (see page 218)
2 tablespoons vegetable oil
1 tablespoon finely chopped fresh
  ginger
1 large onion, finely chopped
¼ teaspoon ground turmeric
4 small potatoes, boiled and cut into
  wedges
1 small green mango, peeled, stoned
  and cut into wedges (optional)
4 small fillets of red bream
1 tablespoon finely chopped
  coriander leaves
sea salt

Put the coconut, fish stock, dried chillies, coriander seeds, tamarind and some salt in a blender and whiz to a smooth paste. Heat half the vegetable oil in a wok, add the ginger and onion and sauté for 5–7 minutes, until the onion is translucent. Add the coconut paste and turmeric and bring to a simmer. Add the potato wedges and the mango, if using, and cook for 6–8 minutes over a low heat. Taste and adjust the seasoning.

Season the bream with salt. Heat the remaining oil in a large frying pan, add the bream and fry over a medium heat for just 1 minute per side, until lightly coloured. Add the partially cooked fish to the sauce and simmer for 3–4 minutes to complete the cooking. Sprinkle over the chopped coriander and serve with boiled or steamed rice.

swordfish curry from madras ━

In India, this curry is made with shark, which tastes delicious. Sadly, we should avoid eating shark now, as it is becoming overfished. Swordfish is very nearly as good.

Alternative fish
haddock, halibut, turbot

SERVES 4

3 tablespoons vegetable oil
2 teaspoons coriander seeds
8 cloves
½ teaspoon black peppercorns
200g fresh coconut, grated (see page 216), or 3 tablespoons desiccated coconut
2 onions, thinly sliced and deep-fried (see page 202)
1 onion, chopped
1 tablespoon Ginger-Garlic Paste (see page 202)
1 teaspoon finely chopped green chilli
100g coriander leaves, ground to a paste in a food processor with a little water
1 teaspoon red chilli powder
1 teaspoon ground turmeric
500g boneless swordfish fillet, cut into cubes
sea salt

Heat half the oil in a frying pan and add the coriander seeds, cloves and peppercorns. As the spices start to splutter, add the grated coconut, saving 1 tablespoon of coconut to garnish. Sauté the mixture until light golden brown, then add the fried onions and remove from the heat. Transfer to a food processor or blender, add a little water and whiz to a paste. Set aside.

Heat the remaining oil in a separate pan, add the chopped onion and fry over a medium heat for 4–5 minutes, until lightly coloured. Stir in the ginger-garlic paste and green chilli and sauté for 3 minutes. Add the coriander paste, chilli powder, turmeric and some salt and stir well. Add the fish and cook over a low heat for 3–4 minutes. Stir in 100ml water and simmer for 3–5 minutes, until the fish turns opaque. Finally, stir in the coconut-onion paste and cook for a further 3–4 minutes. Remove from the heat and garnish with the reserved grated coconut. Serve with boiled rice.

FISH – INDIAN STYLE

mangalore fish curry with tomatoes and ginger ～

MEEN GASSI

I've suggested bass or bream here but the good thing about recipes such as this is that you could use less illustrious fish, like herring, plaice, lemon sole or brill, or even grander ones, such as turbot, monkfish or John Dory. Salmon works very well too. The secret lies in cooking the sauce to perfection and finishing the fish off in a hot oven.

SERVES 4

2 onions, roughly chopped
6 tablespoons vegetable oil
8 curry leaves
1 tablespoon Ginger-Garlic Paste
  (see page 202)
½ teaspoon ground turmeric
3 tablespoons Tamarind Pulp
  (see page 218)
100ml coconut milk
2 tablespoons chopped coriander
  leaves
4 small fillets of sea bass or bream
  (about 125g each)
2 tablespoons rice flour
sea salt and freshly ground black
  pepper

For the masala paste
4 dried red chillies, soaked in 50ml
  white wine vinegar for at least
  2 hours, or overnight
2 teaspoons cumin seeds
1 teaspoon coriander seeds
1 teaspoon mustard seeds
½ teaspoon poppy seeds
2 green cardamom pods

Put all the ingredients for the masala in a blender or food processor and process to a smooth paste, then set aside.

Blend the onions to a paste in a food processor. Tip them into a piece of muslin and squeeze to get rid of the liquid; you should be left with a thick onion pulp.

Heat half the oil in a wok, add the onion pulp and curry leaves and cook until light pink. Add the masala paste and the ginger-garlic paste and cook over a medium heat for 5–7 minutes. Stir in the turmeric, cook for 2 minutes and then add the tamarind, coconut milk, coriander leaves and 50ml water. Simmer for 2–3 minutes, then remove from the heat and keep warm.

Season the fish fillets and roll them in the rice flour to coat. Heat the remaining oil in a large frying pan, add the fish and fry for 1 minute on each side, until golden. Transfer to an oven preheated to 180°C/Gas Mark 4 and cook for 4–5 minutes.

Place the fish on 4 serving plates and spoon the sauce to the side. Serve with a salad or boiled rice.

mumbai fish pizza ⟶

This recipe is a cheeky dig at the stylish folk of Mumbai. Mumbai is quite a trendsetter in India and Italian food is all the rage there at the moment. However, Mumbai wallahs have their own way of cooking Italian food – after all, what do Italians know about Mumbai palates!

SERVES 4

200g white fish fillets (such as pollack or whiting) or mackerel
3 tablespoons vegetable oil
4 tablespoons Spicy Indian Ketchup (see page 209)
4 medium-sized naan breads (bought ones are fine)
1 teaspoon finely chopped garlic
½ teaspoon red chilli flakes
½ teaspoon coriander seeds
¼ teaspoon cumin seeds
1 red onion, sliced
2 tomatoes, sliced
1 red apple, cored and sliced
1 mango, peeled, stoned and diced
1 teaspoon finely chopped fresh ginger
juice and grated zest of 1 lime
a pinch of powdered dried fenugreek leaves
10 coriander sprigs
1 teaspoon dried mango powder
a pinch of garam masala
sea salt and freshly ground black pepper

For the topping
3 tablespoons grated Cheddar cheese
1 tablespoon chopped coriander leaves
1 teaspoon finely chopped green chilli
4 dollops of thick yoghurt

Season the fish fillets with salt and pepper. Heat 2 tablespoons of the oil in a frying pan, add the fish and fry for 3–5 minutes on each side. Drain on kitchen paper, then break into chunks and set aside.

Spread the spicy tomato ketchup over the naan breads and put them on a baking sheet. Place in an oven preheated to 180°C/ Gas Mark 4 and bake for 2 minutes, until they are crisp and the surface is sealed. Remove from the oven and set aside.

Heat the remaining vegetable oil in a pan, add the garlic, red chilli, coriander seeds and cumin seeds and sauté over a medium heat until they start to pop. Stir in the red onion and tomatoes, cook for 2 minutes or until softened, then transfer the mixture to a large bowl. Mix in the cooked fish, apple, mango, ginger, lime juice and zest, fenugreek leaves and coriander sprigs. Sprinkle in the dried mango powder and garam masala and mix well.

Divide the mixture between the naan breads and sprinkle the Cheddar, chopped coriander and chilli on top. Drop a dollop of yoghurt in the centre of each bread and bake in an oven preheated to 200°C/Gas Mark 6 (or under the grill) for 6–8 minutes, until the surface begins to caramelise. Serve immediately.

parathas stuffed with ginger-spiked crab

In India, parathas are often served for breakfast with a mild curry. These can be served like open sandwiches, topped with a little salad.

SERVES 4

2 tablespoons vegetable oil
1 tablespoon finely chopped fresh ginger
1 teaspoon mustard seeds
1 teaspoon finely chopped green chilli
2 teaspoons chopped curry leaves
1 onion, chopped
½ teaspoon ground turmeric or curry powder
1 tablespoon coconut cream
1 tomato, chopped
2 tablespoons finely chopped coriander leaves
400g white crab meat
1 tablespoon lime juice
4 small Parathas (see page 214) or Chapattis (see page 213)
100g mixed salad leaves
sea salt

For the spicy vinaigrette
2 tablespoons olive or vegetable oil
1 tablespoon white wine vinegar
½ teaspoon finely chopped garlic
½ teaspoon cumin seeds, toasted in a dry frying pan and then ground
½ teaspoon red chilli flakes
a pinch of sugar

Heat the oil in a frying pan, add the ginger and sauté for 1 minute. Stir in the mustard seeds, then as they begin to pop, add the green chilli, curry leaves and onion. Sauté until the onion is translucent, then add the turmeric and stir well. Add the coconut cream, tomato and chopped coriander, bring to a simmer and then stir in the crab meat. Remove from the heat and add the lime juice.

Whisk together all the ingredients for the vinaigrette and season with salt. Toss the salad leaves with the vinaigrette. Spread the crab mixture on the parathas and garnish with the dressed salad leaves. Serve immediately.

seafood frittata —

Frittata, or tortilla as it's called in Spain, is a great favourite of mine, but I couldn't resist the opportunity to spice it up. So here's a very simple Indian-style seafood frittata – you can be as creative or lavish as you like with it.

SERVES 6

500ml Fish Stock (see page 203)
200g white fish fillet, such as whiting, cod or pollack
2 tablespoons vegetable oil
1 small green chilli, chopped
½ teaspoon finely chopped fresh ginger
1 large onion, thinly sliced
400g potatoes, peeled and cut into batons about 5cm x 1cm x 1cm
100g shrimps or small prawns
100g white crab meat
8 sun-dried tomatoes
8 large eggs
¼ teaspoon red chilli powder
¼ teaspoon ground coriander
¼ teaspoon ground turmeric
3 tablespoons finely chopped coriander leaves
sea salt

Bring the fish stock to the boil in a pan and then reduce the heat to a simmer. Add the fish fillet and poach gently for about 3 minutes, until just cooked. Remove the fish from the stock and leave until cool enough to handle, then flake the flesh, discarding the skin and any bones.

Heat the oil in a deep 23cm frying pan, preferably a non-stick one. Add the green chilli and ginger, sauté for 1 minute and then add the sliced onion. Sauté over a medium heat for 3–5 minutes, until translucent, then add the potatoes. Stir well and cook for 25–30 minutes, stirring occasionally, until the potatoes are just cooked but not coloured. Add the flaked fish, shrimps or prawns, crab meat and sun-dried tomatoes.

Lightly beat the eggs with the red chilli, ground coriander, turmeric, chopped coriander and some salt, then pour the mixture into the pan. Reduce the heat to medium-low and cook for 12–15 minutes, until almost set. Put the pan under a hot grill for 2–3 minutes, until the omelette is just set and the top is lightly coloured. Serve warm or at room temperature, cut into wedges.

ROASTED SKATE WINGS WITH AVOCADO, MELON AND RED BEAN SALAD ~

MALVANI MASALAE KI MACHCHI

If you buy large skate wings, this makes a hearty family meal. The salad might seem an unusual combination of ingredients but they happen to be my favourite comfort food.

Alternative fish
any firm white fish, such as turbot, kingfish, halibut, cod

SERVES 4

1 teaspoon Malvani Masala
  (see page 204)
4 skate wings
50g butter
½ tablespoon chopped mint
sea salt
lime slices or wedges, to serve

For the salad
2 avocados, peeled, stoned and diced
½ Cantaloupe melon, peeled, deseeded and diced
100g canned red kidney beans, drained and rinsed
½ red onion, thinly sliced
1 Dutch red chilli, finely chopped
1 tablespoon olive oil
1 tablespoon lime juice
sea salt and freshly ground black pepper

Sprinkle the masala over both sides of the skate wings. Melt the butter in a large, heavy-based roasting tin on top of the stove. Add the skate wings and lightly brown them on both sides. Sprinkle with salt, then transfer to an oven preheated to 200°C/ Gas Mark 6 and roast for 10 minutes.

Meanwhile, mix all the salad ingredients together and divide between 4 plates. Place the roasted wings on top of the salad and sprinkle with the mint. Serve straight away, with the lime.

seafood tart ~

Seafood tarts are very common in the West but not often seen in India. I like to make them with crab, prawns, shrimps and smoked or cured fish. The only difference is that I love my spices, so they feature in this recipe, too. Serve with a rocket and tomato salad.

SERVES 4

450ml whole milk
300g undyed smoked haddock or cod fillet
1 tablespoon vegetable oil
1 garlic clove, crushed
¼ teaspoon cumin seeds
1 onion, sliced
a pinch of red chilli flakes
a pinch of ground turmeric
4 spring onions, sliced
5–6 sun-dried tomatoes, diced
100g shrimps
100g white crab meat
2 eggs
2 egg yolks
300ml single cream
sea salt

For the pastry
200g plain flour
½ teaspoon sea salt
75g butter, diced
1 tablespoon vegetable oil
2–3 tablespoons iced water

For the pastry, sift the flour and salt into a bowl, add the butter and rub it in with your fingertips until the mixture resembles fine breadcrumbs. Gradually mix in the oil and enough iced water to form a dough. Roll the pastry out on a lightly floured surface and use to line a 21cm loose-bottomed tart tin with sides 3.5cm deep. Leave a little excess pastry overhanging the sides of the tin, as it will shrink during cooking. Prick the base of the pastry case with a fork and then chill for 20–30 minutes. Cover the base and sides with a sheet of baking parchment and fill with baking beans. Place the tart on a baking sheet in an oven preheated to 200°C/Gas Mark 6 and bake for 10–12 minutes, until beginning to colour lightly. Remove the beans and paper, then return the tart to the oven for 5 minutes. With a sharp knife, trim the edges of the pastry so that they are level with the top of the tin. Reduce the oven temperature to 180°C/Gas Mark 4.

Pour the milk into a pan and bring to a simmer. Add the smoked haddock or cod and poach for 3–5 minutes, then remove from the pan. When the fish is cool enough to handle, flake the flesh, discarding the skin and bones. Strain the poaching liquid and set aside.

In another pan, heat the oil and sauté the garlic and cumin seeds. When the seeds crackle, add the onion, red chilli flakes and turmeric and cook until the onion is translucent. Mix in the spring onions, sun-dried tomatoes, shrimps, crab meat and flaked fish.

Whisk the eggs and egg yolks together, then mix in the cream and 150ml of the fish poaching milk. Spoon the fish mixture into the pastry case and spread evenly. Slowly pour in the egg mixture and bake in the oven at 180°C/Gas Mark 4 for about 35 minutes, until the filling is risen and golden brown. Allow to cool for 10–15 minutes, then remove from the tin.

SOU*th* INDIaN SEA*food* COUSCOUS —

South Indians are quite big on seafood and semolina. They make a kind of savoury porridge out of semolina that plays a similar role to couscous in their diet. However, to keep things simpler, I have used couscous in this recipe.

SERVES 4

2 tablespoons vegetable oil
1 bay leaf
2.5cm piece of cinnamon stick
1 star anise
10 curry leaves
2 onions, chopped
1 teaspoon ground coriander
1 teaspoon ground turmeric
½ teaspoon red chilli powder
500g tomatoes, chopped
150g peeled shrimps or prawns
400g mixed fish fillets, such as grey mullet and red snapper, cut into 5cm pieces
2 tablespoons chopped coriander leaves
sea salt
coriander sprigs, to garnish

For the couscous
2 tablespoons vegetable oil
½ teaspoon mustard seeds
½ teaspoon cumin seeds
20 curry leaves
1 tablespoon finely chopped fresh ginger
1 onion, chopped
2 tablespoons raisins
350ml vegetable stock
300g couscous
1 tablespoon sunflower seeds
1 tablespoon pine nuts or peanuts, lightly toasted in a dry frying pan
1 tablespoon finely chopped coriander leaves
1 tablespoon lemon juice
½ teaspoon grated lemon zest

Heat the oil in a pan, add the bay leaf, cinnamon stick and star anise and sauté for a minute, until the spices sizzle. Add the curry leaves and onions and sauté until the onions are beginning to turn golden. Stir in the ground spices and chopped tomatoes and cook until the tomatoes melt to make a sauce. Add the shrimps or prawns and cook for 2–4 minutes. Finally add the fish and cook for 3–5 minutes, until it is just done. Season to taste and remove from the heat. Sprinkle in the chopped coriander and keep warm.

For the couscous, heat the oil in a pan, add the mustard and cumin seeds and sauté until they pop. Add the curry leaves, ginger and onion and sauté until the onion is translucent. Add the raisins and stock and bring to the boil. Reduce the heat and add the couscous. Mix well, cover the pan and cook gently for 5 minutes, until the liquid has been absorbed. Mix in all the remaining ingredients and remove from the heat.

To serve, put 2 large spoonfuls of couscous on each plate and pour 2 ladlefuls of fish in tomato sauce on top. Garnish with the coriander sprigs.

swordfish strogAnoff ⟶

This is, of course, a recreation of the famous Russian dish. However, I have not only substituted fish for meat but also added some spice. I am not sure what Russian gourmets will make of this but I refuse to worry about it – as long as I am not forced to play Russian roulette!

Alternative fish
turbot, halibut, red snapper

SERVES 4

500g swordfish, cut into 5cm batons
2 tablespoons plain flour
2–3 tablespoons vegetable oil

For the sauce
2 tablespoons vegetable oil
1 teaspoon finely chopped garlic
1 teaspoon finely chopped green chilli
6–8 curry leaves
1 onion, thinly sliced
200g shiitake mushrooms, sliced
1 tablespoon white wine
1 courgette, cut into 5cm batons
200ml single cream
100ml double cream
a pinch of garam masala
1 tablespoon finely chopped
    coriander leaves
sea salt
Boiled Rice (see page 211), to serve

Dust the swordfish batons lightly with the flour. Heat the oil in a frying pan and sauté the fish briefly on both sides until lightly coloured. Remove from the pan and set aside.

For the sauce, heat the oil in a shallow saucepan, add the garlic and chilli and sauté until the garlic turns light golden. Add the curry leaves and onion and sauté until the onion is translucent. Stir in the mushrooms and sauté over a medium-high heat until lightly coloured. Pour in the wine and simmer until it has evaporated. Add the courgette fingers and sauté for a minute, until lightly coloured, then add the single and double creams. Bring to the boil and simmer for 3–4 minutes. Add the fish to the sauce and simmer for another 3–4 minutes, until it is cooked through. Remove from the heat, sprinkle over the chopped coriander and serve with basmati rice.

FISH – INDIAN STYLE

mackerel fillets with mango and coconut sauce ~

ALLEPPEY MEEN KARI

I often make the easiest fish curries possible. Fish is such a delicate ingredient that it has to be cooked with precision. This recipe is very simple, yet utterly delicious. I prefer to cook the fish separately under the grill, but the tradition, as always, is to cook it in the sauce.

Alternative fish
sea bass, red snapper, herrings

SERVES 4

4 medium mackerel, filleted, pin bones removed
2 tablespoons vegetable oil
½ teaspoon ground turmeric
sea salt
rocket leaves, to garnish

For the mango and coconut sauce
flesh from ½ coconut, grated (see page 216)
¼ teaspoon red chilli powder
1 teaspoon ground turmeric
1 small mango, peeled, stoned and diced
1 tomato, diced
10 curry leaves

For the seasoning
1 tablespoon vegetable or coconut oil
¼ teaspoon mustard seeds
¼ teaspoon fenugreek seeds
10 curry leaves

Rub the mackerel fillets with the oil, turmeric and some salt and set aside for 10 minutes.

Meanwhile, for the sauce, put the coconut, chilli powder, turmeric, mango and tomato in a food processor or blender and process to a paste. Transfer the mixture to a pan, add 50ml water and bring to a simmer. Stir in the curry leaves and simmer slowly for 4–5 minutes.

For the seasoning, heat the oil in a small pan and sauté the mustard seeds, fenugreek seeds and curry leaves over a medium-high heat until they pop. Add this seasoning to the sauce and simmer for 2–3 minutes.

Put the fish on a lightly oiled baking tray and grill under a high heat for 2–3 minutes on each side, until just cooked through.

Divide the sauce between 4 serving plates and put the fish on top. Garnish with rocket leaves and serve with boiled rice.

'I often make the easiest fish curries possible.
Fish is such a delicate ingredient that it
has to be cooked with precision.'

TRY USING HERRING FOR THE *MACKEREL FILLETS WITH
MANGO AND COCONUT SAUCE* RECIPE ON PAGE 119.

mild goan fish curry ∼

CALDINHO

This is a gentler version of the usual fiery Goan fish curry. Goans say this is mild enough for children, but I suggest you taste it first before feeding it to yours. It is best made with red or grey mullet but any fish or seafood will do. The only tough part is that you do need to use fresh coconut – but your hard work will be well rewarded.

SERVES 4

1 tablespoon vegetable oil
1 onion, thinly sliced
a pinch of ground turmeric
a walnut-sized piece of tamarind,
    soaked in ½ cup warm water to
    make a pulp (see page 218)
¼ teaspoon ground cloves
¼ teaspoon ground cinnamon
4 red or grey mullet fillets
sea salt and freshly ground black
    pepper
sprigs of coriander, to garnish

For the masala paste
flesh from 1 coconut, grated
    (see page 216)
1 tablespoon finely chopped fresh
    ginger
1 teaspoon coriander seeds
8 black peppercorns
2 green chillies
8 garlic cloves
1 teaspoon rice (uncooked)

Put all the ingredients for the masala paste in a food processor or blender and blend to a smooth paste. Put it in a piece of muslin or a fine tea towel and squeeze into a bowl to extract the thick, spicy coconut milk. Set aside. Turn the masala paste out of the cloth into a bowl, add a cup of hot water and mix well. Squeeze again, into a separate bowl from the thick coconut milk; this time you will end up with thin spicy coconut milk.

Heat the oil in a pan, add the onion and fry until golden brown. Add the turmeric, then pour in the thin coconut milk and bring to a simmer. Pour the tamarind pulp and its soaking liquid through a sieve into the pan, then stir in the ground cloves and cinnamon and simmer for 3–4 minutes. Add the fish fillets and simmer for a further 3–4 minutes, until almost cooked. Now add the thick coconut milk and correct the seasoning with salt and pepper. Bring to a simmer and remove from the heat. Serve garnished with coriander sprigs, accompanied by boiled rice or red Goan rice.

chutney fish steamed with green spice paste and wrapped in banana leaf ~

Traditionally, the fish in this recipe is wrapped in banana leaf and steamed. However, you can also wrap it in foil and bake in a hot oven (220°C/Gas Mark 7) for 12–15 minutes.

SERVES 4

4 x 175g fish fillets -- hake, pollack, whiting, flounder and dab work well
1 tablespoon lemon juice
1 tablespoon vegetable oil
banana leaf for wrapping the fish
sea salt
2 lemons, cut into wedges, to serve

For the spice paste
100g grated fresh coconut (see page 216)
70g coriander leaves
1 green chilli
2 garlic cloves, roughly chopped
½ teaspoon red chilli powder
1 teaspoon coriander seeds, lightly toasted in a dry frying pan
1 teaspoon cumin seeds, lightly toasted in a dry frying pan
2 tablespoons lemon juice
1 tablespoon vegetable oil
1 teaspoon sugar

Rub the fish with the lemon juice, oil and some salt, then set aside while you make the spice paste.

Put all the ingredients for the spice paste in a food processor or blender, season with salt and process until smooth. Coat the fish with the spice paste and set aside for 30 minutes. Wrap each fish fillet in a piece of banana leaf to make a parcel, then place in a steamer and cook for 12–15 minutes.

Remove from the steamer, cut open each parcel and serve with the lemon wedges and a leafy salad.

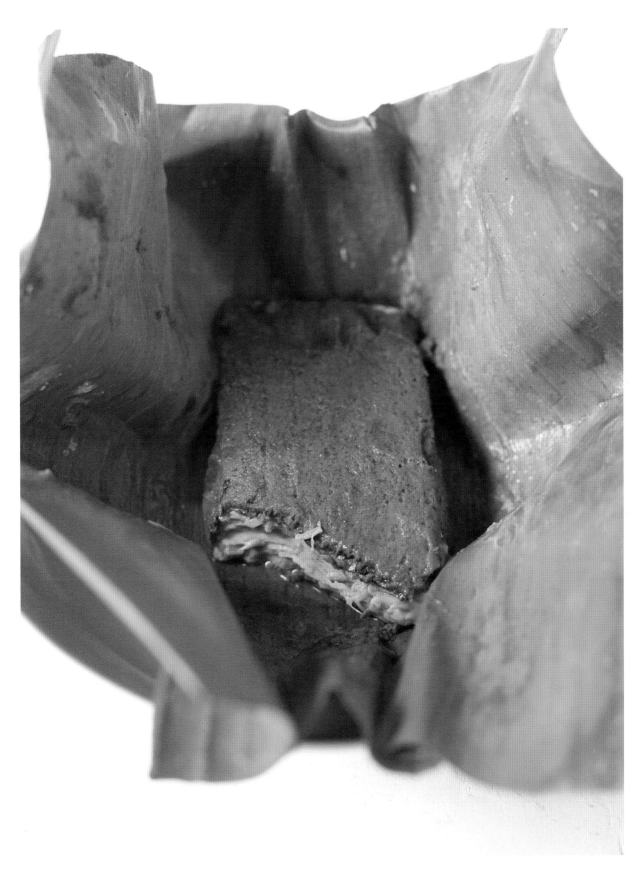

FISH – INDIAN STYLE

easy *fish* MASALA *with* warm tomato and onion salad

This is one of the easiest recipes to make using spices. Fish such as dab and flounder are not rated very highly in the culinary charts but they taste great and, thanks to their abundance, can be enjoyed without guilt. I like to use plenty of ginger-garlic paste in the fish marinade but if you find it too strong, just omit it.

SERVES 4

2 tablespoons lemon juice
1 tablespoon Ginger-Garlic Paste
   (see page 202)
about 1kg fish, such as dab, flounder, brill or plaice, cut into fillets or steaks
5 tablespoons vegetable oil
1 large onion, sliced
2 tomatoes, sliced
½ teaspoon red chilli powder
½ teaspoon ground coriander
½ teaspoon ground turmeric
½ teaspoon ground cumin
1 tablespoon finely chopped fresh ginger
1 tablespoon finely chopped coriander leaves
sea salt
1 lemon, cut into wedges, to serve

Mix together the lemon juice, ginger-garlic paste and some salt and rub them over the fish. Set aside to marinate for 5 minutes.

Heat 4 tablespoons of the oil in a large frying pan, add the fish and fry over a medium heat until just done (the cooking time will depend on whether you are using fillets or steaks). Remove from the heat and keep warm.

Heat the remaining oil in a separate pan, add the onion and sauté for 3–5 minutes, until lightly coloured. Add the tomatoes and sauté for 2 minutes. Stir in all the ground spices and cook for 4–5 minutes. Finally add the ginger and coriander, mix well and remove from the heat.

Divide the sauce between 4 warm plates, place the fish on top and serve with the lemon wedges.

deep-fried john dory with garlic and cumin peas ～

Fish and mushy peas with an Indian twist. My interpretation of Britain's national dish is immensely popular at Benares, and very easy to make at home. Blitzing the peas in a food processor and frying them briefly, rather than boiling, means they retain their vivid colour.

SERVES 2

vegetable oil for deep-frying
2 John Dory fillets, cut into three
  strips each
Spicy Indian Ketchup (see page 209),
  to serve

For the batter
6 tablespoons gram flour
4 tablespoons rice flour (ground rice)
a pinch of sea salt
½ teaspoon red chilli powder
1 teaspoon ajwain seeds
sparkling water

For the garlic and cumin peas
1 tablespoon vegetable oil
1 teaspoon cumin seeds
2 garlic cloves, chopped
100g frozen peas, thawed
sea salt

To make the batter, put the gram flour, rice flour, salt, chilli powder and ajwain seeds in a bowl and gradually stir in enough sparkling water to give a thick, pouring consistency; it should be thick enough to coat the back of the spoon.

Heat the vegetable oil to 180°C in a deep-fat fryer or a large, deep saucepan. Dip the fish in the batter, let any excess drain off, then fry for 4–5 minutes, until golden and crisp. Drain on kitchen paper.

While the fish is frying, cook the peas. Heat the vegetable oil in a small pan, add the cumin seeds and cook for a few seconds, until they start to crackle. Add the garlic and cook until golden. Blitz the peas very briefly in a food processor to break them down a little, then add to the pan and fry for just a minute or two, until tender but still brightly coloured. Season to taste. Serve the fish with the peas and spicy ketchup – and some chips, if you like.

FISH – INDIAN STYLE

blackened grilled tilapia with pineapple salad

Tilapia farming has recently started in the UK, making it much more readily available. Although the farmed fish is not as good as wild African tilapia, it comes pretty close.

Alternative fish
red snapper, John Dory, plaice, lemon
  sole

SERVES 4

4 x 400g tilapia, cleaned

For the tamarind glaze
1 teaspoon cumin seeds
1 teaspoon coriander seeds
1 teaspoon fennel seeds
6–8 garlic cloves, sliced, deep-fried in
  hot oil until golden and then
  crushed in a mortar and pestle
4 tablespoons Tamarind Pulp
  (see page 218)
2 tablespoons vegetable oil
1 tablespoon brown sugar
½ teaspoon red chilli powder
1 teaspoon Ginger Paste (see page 202)
sea salt

For the pineapple salad
1 tablespoon vegetable oil
1 teaspoon mustard seeds
200g pineapple, diced
1 red chilli, sliced
a pinch of ground turmeric
juice and grated zest of 1 lime
10 large mint leaves, chopped
a pinch of sugar
sea salt and freshly ground black
  pepper

First make the tamarind glaze. Toast all the seeds in a dry frying pan and then grind them to a powder. Put the seeds in a pan with all the remaining glaze ingredients and bring to a simmer. Cook, stirring occasionally, until the mixture becomes a thick paste and is shiny on the surface.

For the salad, heat the oil in a pan over a medium heat and add the mustard seeds. When they start to pop, add all the rest of the ingredients and cook for a couple of minutes. Remove from the heat and leave to cool.

Make 3 diagonal slashes on both sides of each fish and then brush with the tamarind glaze. Place under a very hot grill and cook for 2–3 minutes on each side, until just done. Serve with the pineapple salad.

FISH – INDIAN STYLE

bubble and squeak with leftover fish

Cooking with leftovers has become the norm for me at home. My wife, Deepti, cooks for the kids during the week and the leftovers are piled in the fridge for me to deal with at the weekend. It forces me to be creative, and this is one of my most successful inventions.

SERVES 4

about 700g leftover mashed potatoes
about 400g cooked fish (in any form
   – fried, curried, poached, etc.),
   broken into flakes
5 tablespoons vegetable oil
½ teaspoon cumin seeds
1 garlic clove, chopped
1 onion, chopped
½ teaspoon ground turmeric
½ teaspoon ground coriander
1 teaspoon finely chopped fresh
   ginger
1 green chilli chopped
200g kale, chopped
sea salt and freshly ground black
   pepper
Mint and Coriander Chutney, to
   serve (see page 207)

Mix the potatoes and fish together in a large bowl and set aside.

Heat 2 tablespoons of the oil in a non-stick frying pan, add the cumin and garlic and sauté until lightly coloured. Add the onion and sauté until translucent, then stir in the turmeric, coriander, ginger, chilli and kale. Cook until the kale wilts, then tip the mixture into the bowl with the fish and potato and mix well. Season with salt and pepper, then shape into large cakes.

Heat the remaining oil in a large frying pan, add the bubble and squeak cakes and fry them lightly on both sides until browned. Serve immediately, with the chutney.

steamed pollack cakes with tomato, coriander and peanut chutney —

IDLI

Idli are a popular South Indian snack made with rice and lentils, but fish, works well too. Traditionally they are served with *sambhar*, a lentil dish, but I like to serve them with chutney.

Alternative fish
cod, ling, whiting

SERVES 4

600g pollack fillet, skinned, pin bones
   removed
2 tablespoons vegetable oil
1 teaspoon mustard seeds
5 curry leaves, chopped
1 teaspoon finely chopped fresh ginger
¼ teaspoon finely chopped green
   chilli
1 tablespoon roasted channa lentils
   (optional)
1 egg white
1 tablespoon single cream
sea salt
a few fried curry leaves, to garnish
   (optional)

**For the tomato, coriander and
   peanut chutney**
2 tablespoons vegetable oil
1 teaspoon mustard seeds
½ teaspoon cumin seeds
8–9 curry leaves
50g unsalted peanuts, crushed
1 onion, chopped
½ teaspoon red chilli powder
½ teaspoon ground coriander
½ teaspoon ground turmeric
300g tomatoes, chopped
1 tablespoon lemon juice
2 tablespoons palm sugar or brown
   sugar

First make the chutney. Heat the oil in a saucepan, add the mustard seeds, cumin seeds and curry leaves and sauté until they pop. Add the crushed peanuts and onion and sauté until the onion is translucent. Stir in the red chilli powder, coriander and turmeric, then add the tomatoes. Cook over a medium heat for 10–12 minutes, until thickened slightly. Stir in the lemon juice, sugar and some salt and cook for a further 3–4 minutes. Remove from the heat and set aside.

To make the idli, put the pollack fillet in a food processor and pulse until it becomes a smooth paste. Heat the oil in a small pan, add the mustard seeds, curry leaves, ginger, green chilli and channa lentils and sauté over a medium heat until the spices begin to pop. Add this mixture to the fish, together with the egg white and cream. Mix well and season with salt. Shape the mixture into cakes about 5cm in diameter. Arrange them in a steamer lined with banana leaves or baking parchment and steam for 5–7 minutes, until cooked through. Serve the fish cakes with the chutney, garnishing with a few fried curry leaves, if liked.

FISH – INDIAN STYLE

kingfish vindaloo ~

Traditionally made with pork, vindaloo came to Goa by way of Portugal, and has become Indian thanks to the use of spices and chillies. It should never contain potatoes but should include lots of garlic and vinegar – the name comes from the Portuguese, *vinho de alho*, referring to vinegar and garlic.

A vindaloo can vary in colour from dark brown to deep red, depending on the quantity of chillies used. I prefer to use as few as possible, so my sauce generally turns out to be a brownish colour. For the photo opposite, I fried the fish separately and served it on, rather than in, the sauce, so it is not masked by it – you can do it whichever way you prefer.

Alternative fish
mackerel, turbot, monkfish, swordfish

SERVES 6–8

3 tablespoons vegetable oil
2.5cm piece of cinnamon stick
2 cloves
1 bay leaf
1 onion, sliced
2 tomatoes, chopped
250ml warm water
800g kingfish steaks
1 tablespoon white wine vinegar
sea salt
coriander leaves, to garnish
Chutney Rice (see page 211), to serve

For the vindaloo paste
3 tablespoons vegetable oil
1 onion, chopped
20g dried red Kashmiri chillies,

soaked in hot water overnight
4 green cardamom pods
5cm piece of cinnamon stick
4 cloves
½ teaspoon coriander seeds
½ teaspoon cumin seeds
½ teaspoon ground turmeric
2.5cm piece of fresh ginger
2 tablespoons chopped garlic
a walnut-sized piece of tamarind pulp
  (see page 218)
1 teaspoon brown sugar
2 tablespoons white wine vinegar

First make the vindaloo paste. Heat the oil in a small pan, add the onion and sauté for 8–10 minutes, until soft and light brown. Remove from the heat and set aside. Drain the chillies and squeeze out the water. Grind the spices to a powder and mix with the turmeric. Put the chillies, fried onion, ginger, garlic, tamarind pulp, sugar, vinegar and ground spices in a food processor or blender and process to a paste. (This makes more than you will need for this recipe, but if you mix in 2 tablespoons of vegetable oil the paste will keep in the fridge for weeks.)

Heat the oil in a large pan, add the cinnamon, cloves, bay leaf and onion and cook until the onion is richly caramelised. Add 4 tablespoons of the vindaloo paste and sauté for 3–4 minutes. Add the tomatoes and cook over a low heat for 6–8 minutes, adding the water a little at a time to keep the sauce moist.

Season the kingfish steaks with salt, add them to the sauce and simmer gently for 5–7 minutes, until the fish is cooked through. Stir in the vinegar, garnish with the coriander and serve with the chutney rice.

FISH – INDIAN STYLE

*fi*sh quene*ll*es in a curry sauce

MACHCHI KI KOFTA CURRY

Fish kofta is a popular supper in Indian households near the coast. The curry sauce varies from mild to hot, according to the region. This one is full of aromas and flavours. I like to use farmed cod but virtually any fish will be suitable.

SERVES 4

400g farmed cod fillets, skinned, pin
   bones removed
1 egg
1 teaspoon cumin seeds, toasted in a
   dry frying pan and then ground
1 teaspoon finely chopped fresh
   ginger
½ teaspoon coarsely crushed dried
   red chilli
a pinch of freshly grated nutmeg
1 tablespoon finely chopped
   coriander leaves
2 tablespoons lime juice
grated zest of 1 lime
120ml double cream
sea salt

For the sauce
3 tablespoons coconut oil or
   vegetable oil
100g desiccated coconut
1 teaspoon fennel seeds
½ onion, finely chopped, plus 1 onion,
   finely sliced
1 teaspoon fenugreek seeds
1 teaspoon mustard seeds
25 curry leaves
4 green chillies, chopped
1 tablespoon Ginger-Garlic Paste
   (see page 202)
2 tablespoons ground coriander
1 teaspoon red chilli powder

½ teaspoon ground turmeric
100g green mango, peeled, stoned
   and sliced into thin strips
200ml coconut milk

Put the fish fillets in a food processor with the egg, cumin seeds, ginger, red chilli, nutmeg, coriander leaves, lime juice and zest and blend to a smooth paste. Transfer to a bowl set over a larger bowl containing iced water and gently stir in the cream a little at a time to thicken the mixture. When it has all been incorporated, remove the bowl from the bowl of iced water, cover and chill for 30–40 minutes.

Meanwhile, make the sauce. Heat a tablespoon of the oil in a saucepan, add the desiccated coconut, fennel seeds and finely chopped onion and sauté for 4–5 minutes, until the onion is translucent. Remove from the pan and process to a smooth paste in a blender.

Now heat the remaining oil in the pan and sauté the fenugreek seeds, mustard seeds and curry leaves until aromatic. Add the sliced onion and fry until translucent, then add the green chillies and the ginger-garlic paste. Sauté for 2 minutes, then add the ground spices and half the mango. Cook for 5–7 minutes, then stir in the coconut paste, the coconut milk and the rest of the mango. Simmer gently for 5 minutes, then remove from the heat and keep warm.

Bring a wide, shallow pan of lightly salted water to the boil and keep it at a gentle simmer. Shape the fish mixture into walnut-sized balls and drop them into the simmering water a few at a time. Poach for 3–4 minutes, turning them over half way through. When they are done, the fish will turn opaque and the balls will feel firmer to the touch. Remove with a slotted spoon and drain on kitchen paper. Keep warm while you cook the rest.

To serve, divide the quenelles between 4 dishes and pour the sauce over. Accompany with a bowl of rice.

Spice-Roasted Barramundi

KHADE MASALAE KI BARRAMUNDI

Barramundi's flavour comes alive with spices. This fish has got so much character that it needs strong tastes to work with. It's a great fish for a barbecue. I have used simple spices here but you could pick your own favourites and create your own combination.

Alternative fish
red mullet, red snapper, carp,
  mackerel

SERVES 2

2 barramundi, cleaned
1 teaspoon Garlic Paste (see page 202)
2 tablespoons vegetable oil
1 teaspoon crushed coriander seeds
1 teaspoon crushed fennel seeds
1 teaspoon red chilli flakes
½ teaspoon freshly ground black
  pepper
juice and grated zest of 1 lemon
1 tablespoon butter, melted
sea salt

To garnish
chopped chives, fennel fronds or
  rosemary
a few slices of lemon

Make 3 slashes on each side of the fish. Mix the garlic paste with 1 tablespoon of the oil, plus the spices, lemon zest, half the lemon juice and some salt. Rub this marinade on the fish. Place the fish in a shallow baking dish, brush them with the melted butter and place in an oven preheated to 220°C/Gas Mark 7. Roast for 20 minutes, turning the fish half way through.

Transfer the fish to a platter and drizzle with the remaining oil and lemon juice. Garnish with chopped chives, fennel leaves or rosemary and a few lemon slices. Serve with a salad.

ROAST *mullet* WITH ROASTED VEGETABLES —

MACHCHI BHUNA

I decided to use grey mullet for this recipe but any large, round fish would be suitable. *Bhuna* is a loose cooking method that involves sautéing, stewing or stir-frying before finishing the dish off in the oven. You can buy jars of sauce labelled bhuna but they have nothing to do with cooking bhuna style.
You could substitute any vegetable you fancy for the peppers, as long as you adjust the cooking time where necessary.

SERVES 4

1 x 2kg grey mullet, scaled and cleaned
1 tablespoon lemon juice
½ teaspoon ground turmeric
½ teaspoon ground coriander
1 tablespoon vegetable oil
sea salt
sprigs of coriander, to garnish

For the sauce
3 tablespoons vegetable oil
1 teaspoon cumin seeds
2 green cardamom pods
1 bay leaf
2 cloves
3 onions, chopped
1 teaspoon Ginger-Garlic Paste
  (see page 202)
2 red peppers, diced
1 green pepper, diced
1 teaspoon ground coriander
1 teaspoon ground turmeric

½ teaspoon garam masala
3 tomatoes, chopped
150ml Fish Stock (see page 203)
1 tablespoon lemon juice

Score the fish with 5 or 6 diagonal slashes on each side, so it cooks well. Mix together the lemon juice, turmeric, coriander and some salt and rub them over the fish. Heat the vegetable oil in a large, heavy-based frying pan and sear the fish briefly on both sides. Remove from the heat and set aside.

To make the sauce, heat the oil in a heavy-based roasting tin, casserole or ovenproof frying pan that is large enough to hold the fish. Add the cumin seeds, cardamom, bay leaf, cloves and onions and cook over a medium heat until the onions are lightly caramelised. Add the ginger-garlic paste and sauté for 2–3 minutes, then add the peppers and all the ground spices. Sauté for 2 minutes, then add the tomatoes. Stir in the fish stock, lemon juice and some salt and bring to a simmer. Add the fish and cook for 3–5 minutes, turning the fish a few times. Transfer to an oven preheated to 200°C/Gas Mark 6 and bake, uncovered, for 25–30 minutes, until the fish is completely cooked. Serve garnished with coriander sprigs and accompanied by some naan bread.

BRAISED KINGfish —

VENTHIAM MEEN KARI

Kingfish is really a big mackerel. I have been cooking it for over 20 years now, and find that it is most suited to curries and braises. In coastal India, this fish works better than the local currency.

Alternative fish
sea trout, mackerel, carp

SERVES 4

2 tablespoons vegetable oil
½ teaspoon crushed fenugreek seeds
1 teaspoon mustard seeds,
1 teaspoon chopped garlic
1 onion, finely chopped
1 carrot, finely sliced
1 teaspoon red chilli powder
½ teaspoon ground turmeric
1 teaspoon each fennel seeds and
   cumin seeds, toasted in a dry frying
   pan and then ground
400ml coconut milk
1 tablespoon Tamarind Pulp
   (see page 218)
600g kingfish fillets, skinned
crisp, deep-fried spring onion strips,
   to garnish (optional)

Heat the oil in a large pan, add the fenugreek and mustard seeds and sauté over a medium heat until they pop. Add the garlic and sauté until lightly coloured, then add the onion and carrot and fry until the onion is translucent. Stir in the chilli powder, turmeric, ground cumin and fennel and fry for 1 minute, until the mixture is aromatic. Add the coconut milk and tamarind pulp, bring to the boil and simmer until the sauce has reduced by half. Gently lower the fish fillets into the sauce and simmer, uncovered, for 3–5 minutes, until the fish is cooked. Serve immediately garnished with the deep-fried spring onion strips, if using. It's good accompanied with a watercress salad and some rice.

devilled crabs baked in their shells

I find the UK has some of the best crabs in the world, and the best of all are Cromer crabs. Their meat and juice are second to none. This recipe is an Indian version of traditional devilled crab but without the mustard – I wonder how I can pump up the heat!

SERVES 4

4 dressed Cromer crabs
2 tablespoons vegetable oil
1 onion, sliced
1 teaspoon finely chopped fresh ginger
¼ teaspoon ground turmeric
2 tablespoons Tamarind Pulp (see page 218) or lemon juice
2 tablespoons coconut milk
1 tablespoon coriander leaves
15g fresh breadcrumbs
1 tablespoon melted butter
50g Cheddar cheese, grated (optional)
sea salt

For the spice paste
4 tablespoons grated fresh coconut (see page 216), or 2 tablespoons desiccated coconut
2 dried red chillies
1 teaspoon coriander seeds
5–6 black peppercorns
1 clove

Remove the crab meat from the shells, reserving the shells, and put it in a large bowl.

Toast all the ingredients for the spice paste separately in a dry frying pan over a medium heat, then leave to cool. Grind them together in a food processor, then set aside.

Heat the oil in a frying pan, add the sliced onion and sauté until light brown. Add the ginger and turmeric and sauté for 1 minute, then stir in the crab meat and tamarind or lemon juice. Add the coconut milk and the ground spice paste and cook for 1–2 minutes. Season with salt if necessary, remove from the heat and sprinkle in the coriander.

Spoon the crab mixture back into the shells and lightly level the surface. Mix the breadcrumbs with the melted butter and the grated cheese, if using, and sprinkle evenly over the crab. Place the crabs on a baking tray and bake in an oven preheated to 200°C/Gas Mark 6 for 7–10 minutes, until golden brown on top. Serve with a green salad.

FISH – INDIAN STYLE

GRILLed RED bReaM wITH sPICE rub

This is very much my kind of dish – when I want to entertain, but also to sit and chat with my friends. I love coming up with new combinations of spices, and the spice rub here is a particular favourite. Many other spice blends would work and you can adapt it and use whatever you fancy – it's as easy as that.

Alternative fish
red snapper, John Dory, sea bass, tilapia, barramundi

SERVES 4

4 x 150g red bream fillets
lemon wedges, to serve

For the spice rub
3 tablespoons walnut or olive oil
4 tablespoons chopped coriander leaves
2 garlic cloves, crushed
1 teaspoon coriander seeds, crushed
1 teaspoon cumin seeds, crushed
1 tablespoon lemon juice
1 small green chilli, very finely chopped

For the tomato salad
4 plum tomatoes, chopped
1 tablespoon chopped coriander leaves
1½ teaspoons walnut or olive oil
1 tablespoon walnuts, toasted in a dry frying pan and then lightly crushed
sea salt and freshly ground black pepper

Mix all the ingredients for the spice rub together and season with salt. Line a baking sheet with foil and place the fish fillets on it, skin-side down. Brush the spice rub on the fish. Place under a hot grill for 6–8 minutes, until cooked through and lightly golden. Remove from the heat and keep warm.

Meanwhile, mix together all the ingredients for the tomato salad. Serve the fish with the salad and some lemon wedges.

JUMBO prawns WITH curry leaf powder and mooli and radish salad —

KARUVEPAK YERRA

In southern India, different types of spice powders are prepared to flavour meat, fish and lentils. They are very versatile and can be used with any cooking method. This curry leaf powder is perfect with fish. You won't need all of it for this recipe but it will keep well for 2–3 weeks in an airtight jar. Try mixing it with breadcrumbs and using it to coat meat, fish or vegetables before frying.

Alternative fish
small prawns or even small whole fish such as sardines, with the skin and head removed

SERVES 4

12 headless raw jumbo prawns
1 tablespoon lemon juice
2 tablespoons vegetable oil
50g butter
sea salt and freshly ground black
 pepper
a few fried curry leaves, to garnish
 (optional)

For the curry leaf powder
2 tablespoons vegetable oil
100g curry leaves
2 tablespoons black peppercorns
1 teaspoon cumin seeds
2 tablespoons black gram lentils
1 walnut-sized piece of tamarind
 pulp, without seeds

For the mooli and radish salad
1 small mooli, peeled and sliced
10 radishes, sliced
½ teaspoon cumin seeds, toasted in
 a dry frying pan and then crushed
1½ teaspoons vegetable oil
1 teaspoon lemon juice
sea salt

To make the curry leaf powder, heat the oil in a frying pan, add the curry leaves and fry for 1–2 minutes, until crisp. In a small, dry frying pan, toast the peppercorns, cumin seeds and gram lentils separately over a medium heat until they are slightly dried. Put them in a food processor with the tamarind and fried curry leaves and process to a powder. Leave to cool.

Peel the prawns and, using the point of a sharp knife, remove the dark, intestinal vein running down their backs. Sprinkle the prawns with the lemon juice and some salt and pepper. Heat the oil in a frying pan, add the prawns and fry over a medium heat for 3–4 minutes, until almost cooked through. Melt the butter in a separate pan. Add the prawns to the butter, then add 2 tablespoons of the curry leaf powder and cook over a high heat for 2–3 minutes, spooning the curry butter on top of the prawns. Remove from the pan and drain on kitchen paper. Put all the ingredients for the salad in a bowl and toss well. Serve the prawns accompanied by the salad, garnished with a few fried curry leaves, if liked.

pushing the boat out ~

FISH ‒ INDIAN STYLE

JOHN DORY WITH GREEN SPICE PASTE AND ROASTED TOMATOES

HARI MACHCHI

I have been cooking this recipe for 14 years now and it has pretty much become my signature dish. I devised it when I was experimenting with the quality of John Dory in the UK and it has never swum off my menu!

Alternative fish
red snapper, sea bass, cod, monkfish

SERVES 4

4 x 150g John Dory fillets
2 tablespoons lemon juice
½ teaspoon salt
4 tablespoons vegetable oil
30g enoki mushrooms
a few micro herbs or herb sprigs
2 tablespoons Spicy Vinaigrette
  (see page 110)

For the green spice paste
50g mint leaves
50g coriander leaves
10g piece of fresh ginger, chopped
2 green chillies
1½ teaspoons powdered dried
  fenugreek leaves
2 teaspoons chaat masala
1 teaspoon red chilli powder
½ teaspoon salt
2 tablespoons gram flour
2 tablespoons lemon juice

For the roasted tomatoes
1 tablespoon vegetable oil
¼ teaspoon cumin seeds
½ onion, chopped
4 strings of small tomatoes on the
  vine
½ teaspoon finely chopped fresh
  ginger
½ teaspoon ground coriander
½ teaspoon ground turmeric
½ teaspoon chaat masala
1 tablespoon finely chopped
  coriander leaves
sea salt

To make the green spice paste, put all the ingredients in a food processor with 2 tablespoons of water and whiz to a paste. Transfer to a bowl large enough to hold the fish.

Sprinkle the John Dory fillets with the salt and lemon juice and set aside for 15 minutes to drain off excess moisture. Pat the fish dry, coat it in the spice paste and leave to marinate for 40 minutes.

To cook the tomatoes, heat the oil in an ovenproof frying pan, add the cumin seeds and onion and sauté till translucent. Add the tomatoes on the vine and sprinkle over the spices and some salt. Transfer the pan to an oven preheated to 180°C/Gas Mark 4 and roast for 5–7 minutes, until the tomatoes start to wilt. Remove from the oven, sprinkle with the coriander leaves and keep warm.

To cook the fish, heat the oil in a large, ovenproof frying pan. Scrape off excess marinade from the fish fillets and add them to the pan, flesh-side down. Cook for 2 minutes, then turn and fry the other side for 2 minutes. Transfer the pan to the oven for 3–5 minutes to complete the cooking. Remove the fish and drain on kitchen paper.

To serve, put the tomatoes in the centre of each plate and place the John Dory on top. Toss the enoki mushrooms and micro herbs or herb sprigs with the vinaigrette and use to garnish the fish.

ROAST JOHN DORY WITH YELLOW PUMPKIN SOUP ~

TAWAE KI MACHCHI

John Dory has been my favourite fish for many years. I love its firm texture and delicate flavour. This fish requires some kind of sauce or spice to balance the dish and here a lightly spiced pumpkin soup does the job.

Alternative fish
red snapper, sea bass, cod, monkfish

SERVES 4

4 x 150g John Dory fillets
1 tablespoon gram flour
3 tablespoons vegetable oil
sea salt

For the yellow pumpkin soup
3 tablespoons vegetable or olive oil
1 tablespoon grated fresh ginger
1 small green chilli, deseeded and
   finely chopped
1 onion, chopped
500g peeled, deseeded pumpkin,
   roughly chopped
40g caster sugar
50ml dry white wine
400ml vegetable or chicken stock
2 tablespoons double cream (optional)
¼ teaspoon ground cinnamon

For the marinade
1 teaspoon Ginger-Garlic Paste
   (see page 202)
1 teaspoon ajwain seeds
½ teaspoon ground turmeric
¼ teaspoon garam masala
1 teaspoon lemon juice

For the greens
2 teaspoons vegetable or olive oil
1 teaspoon finely chopped garlic
¼ teaspoon crushed black
   peppercorns or red chilli flakes
200g baby spinach leaves or lettuce
   leaves
¼ teaspoon ground turmeric
¼ teaspoon ground coriander

To garnish
coriander or chervil leaves
lightly crushed red (or black)
   peppercorns

First make the soup. Heat the oil in a large pan, add the ginger and chilli and sauté for a minute. Add the onion and sauté for 3–5 minutes, until softened, then add the pumpkin and cook for 3–4 minutes. Stir in the sugar, white wine and some salt and simmer until the wine has reduced by half. Add the stock and the cream, if using, bring to the boil and simmer for 10 minutes or until the pumpkin is tender. Cool slightly and then blend the soup with a stick blender until smooth. Pass though a fine sieve, stir in the cinnamon and keep warm.

Mix together all the ingredients for the marinade and season with salt. Rub the marinade over the fish fillets and set aside for 5 minutes.

Dust the fish with the gram flour. Heat the oil in a large, ovenproof frying pan, add the fish, skin-side down and fry over a medium heat for 3–4 minutes, until the skin is crisp. Flip it over on to the other side and fry for 1 minute. Transfer to an oven preheated to 180°C/Gas Mark 4 for 3–5 minutes to complete the cooking.

Meanwhile, cook the greens. Heat the oil in a frying pan, add the garlic and sauté until light brown. Add the pepper or chilli flakes, plus the spinach or lettuce and the spices. Sauté briefly until the leaves wilt, then season with salt and remove from the heat.

To serve, place the greens in the middle of 4 deep serving plates and pour the soup around them. Place the fish on top of the greens, garnish with coriander or chervil leaves and sprinkle with the crushed red pepper.

goan-style LOBSTER ⁓

LAGUSTA XEC XEC

I love cooking lobster. Its beautiful, sweet flesh goes with almost anything. This is a traditional Goan spice blend but the dish is given a modern British twist by poaching the lobster and then finishing it with melted butter.

SERVES 4

4 live lobsters
3 tablespoons vegetable oil
2 onions, sliced
1 green chilli, finely chopped
½ teaspoon Ginger-Garlic Paste
  (see page 202)
¼ teaspoon ground turmeric
50ml Tamarind Pulp (see page 218)
150ml coconut milk
2 tablespoons finely chopped
  coriander leaves
2 tablespoons butter

For the spice paste
200g fresh coconut, grated (see page 216)
2 dried red chillies
2 tablespoons coriander seeds
1 teaspoon black peppercorns
4 cloves

Put the lobsters in the freezer for 2 hours, until almost frozen – this will render them unconscious. Then add them to a very large pan of boiling salted water and simmer for 2 minutes. Remove from the pan, immerse them in chilled water, then drain. Remove all the meat from the shells, keeping it whole – discard the black intestinal vein that runs down the tail flesh and the stomach sac and gills from the head. The meat will just be blanched, not completely cooked, at this stage.

Next make the spice paste. Lightly toast the grated coconut in a dry frying pan, then tip it on to a plate and leave to cool. Toast the dried chillies, coriander seeds, peppercorns and cloves in the pan for 2 minutes or until lightly coloured, then remove and leave to cool. Put the toasted spices and coconut in a food processor or blender with a few tablespoons of water (or coconut milk) and blend to a smooth paste. Set aside.

Heat 2 tablespoons of the vegetable oil in a wok, add the onions and green chilli and sauté for 5–7 minutes, until light brown. Stir in the ginger-garlic paste and turmeric and sauté for 2–3 minutes. Add the spice paste and cook, stirring, for 2 minutes. Add the tamarind pulp and simmer for 2–3 minutes, then pour in the coconut milk and simmer for 10 minutes. Stir in 2–3 tablespoons of water to adjust the consistency to a thin sauce. Sprinkle in the chopped coriander.

Heat the remaining vegetable oil in a non-stick frying pan and sauté the lobster meat for 3–4 minutes. Add the butter to the pan and let it melt, then spoon it over the lobster to form a light glaze.

Bring the sauce to a simmer.

Traditionally this dish is completed by adding the cooked lobster meat to the sauce, simmering for a minute and then serving. But I like to serve the shiny pink lobster sitting on the beautiful, deep yellow sauce, accompanied by boiled rice or a salad.

grilled salmon with a lime crust

NIMBU KI PARAT KI MACHCHI

Cooking in a curry sauce is not the only way to produce Indian food – you can spice a piece of fish in many ways. Here the salmon is coated in a zesty lime crust and then grilled. The flavours are fresh and well balanced, and it's really easy to make.

Alternative fish
haddock, halibut, plaice, lemon sole, sea trout, Arctic char

SERVES 4

4 x 125g pieces of salmon fillet, skinned
1 tablespoon olive oil
sea salt and freshly ground black pepper

For the lime crust
100g pine nuts, lightly toasted in a dry frying pan
50g fresh breadcrumbs
120g softened butter
1 teaspoon grated lime zest
1 tablespoon lime juice
2 kaffir lime leaves, finely chopped (optional)
a pinch of garam masala

For the tomato sauce
250g plum tomatoes, cut in half
1 teaspoon sherry vinegar
1 tablespoon olive oil
1 teaspoon honey
a pinch of garam masala
3 tablespoons double cream
50g butter, diced

For the grilled salad
½ pineapple, peeled, cored and sliced
2 apples, cored and sliced
2 baby Little Gem lettuces, leaves separated
½ teaspoon chaat masala
1 teaspoon lemon juice

For the crust, roughly chop the nuts and mix with the rest of the ingredients and a pinch of sea salt. Place the mixture between 2 sheets of baking parchment and spread it with the help of a rolling pin until 2mm thick. Place in the freezer. Once it is frozen, cut the crust into 4 pieces the same size as the salmon fillet and return it to the freezer.

For the sauce, whiz the tomatoes, vinegar, oil, honey and garam masala in a blender or food processor. Strain it through a sieve into a pan and bring to the boil. Simmer until slightly reduced, then stir in the cream. Whisk in the butter a few pieces at a time until you have a glossy sauce, then season to taste. Keep warm until required.

To make the grilled salad, toss all the ingredients together in a baking tray and place under a hot grill. Grill for about 3–5 minutes, until the fruit is lightly coloured and the lettuce wilted. Keep warm while you cook the fish.

Season the fish with salt and pepper and drizzle with the oil. Cook under the grill for 4–5 minutes, until firm. Remove, and place the crust on top and then return to the grill for 1–2 minutes to colour the crust lightly.

To serve, divide the grilled salad between 4 plates. Pour the tomato sauce around and place the fish on top.

seared tuna with black trumpet mushroom crust and beetroot pickle ~

KHUMBIWALI TAWAE KI MACHCHI

I saw chef Rick Tramanto cook this recipe at his restaurant in Chicago. It tastes amazing! Tuna stocks are currently depleted in our oceans, but careful conservation is the way forward. For the moment, bluefin tuna is seriously endangered but yellowfin stocks are in better shape. So make fresh tuna an occasional treat and stick to yellowfin.

Fresh black trumpet mushrooms, or black chanterelles, are in season in the summer. With the aid of a good mushroom handbook, they are relatively easy to find in woods, growing mostly under oaks. If you can't get hold of dried black trumpet mushrooms, you can order them online from www.smithy-mushrooms.co.uk.

SERVES 4

600g fresh tuna, cut into 4 logs
100g dried black trumpet mushrooms
 (or other dried wild mushrooms),
 ground to a powder in a spice grinder
1 teaspoon Madras Spice Powder
 (see page 204)
1 tablespoon vegetable oil
sea salt

For the beetroot pickle
1 tablespoon vegetable oil
1 teaspoon finely chopped fresh ginger
1 teaspoon mustard seeds
1 green chilli, chopped
4 raw beetroot, cut into 2.5cm dice
1 tablespoon honey
1 tablespoon caster sugar
200ml white wine vinegar
300ml water

For the butternut squash
2 tablespoons vegetable oil
½ teaspoon onion seeds or mustard
 seeds
1 teaspoon grated fresh ginger
2–3 curry leaves, chopped
300g peeled and deseeded butternut
 squash, cut into 2.5cm dice
¼ teaspoon ground turmeric
¼ teaspoon sugar
1 teaspoon lemon juice

For the mushrooms
1 tablespoon butter
1 teaspoon chopped garlic
6–8 spring onions, sliced on the
 diagonal
50g black trumpet mushrooms

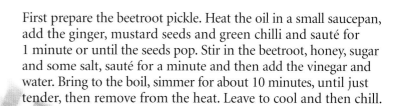

First prepare the beetroot pickle. Heat the oil in a small saucepan, add the ginger, mustard seeds and green chilli and sauté for 1 minute or until the seeds pop. Stir in the beetroot, honey, sugar and some salt, sauté for a minute and then add the vinegar and water. Bring to the boil, simmer for about 10 minutes, until just tender, then remove from the heat. Leave to cool and then chill.

For the butternut squash, heat the oil in a saucepan, add the onion or mustard seeds, ginger and curry leaves and sauté for 1 minute or until the seeds pop. Add the butternut squash, sauté for a minute and then add the turmeric and some salt. Cook on a low heat for 10–12 minutes, until the squash is tender. Stir in the sugar and lemon juice, remove from the heat and keep warm.

For the mushrooms, heat the butter in a small frying pan, add the garlic and fry over a medium heat until golden. Add the spring onions and mushrooms and cook over a high heat for 2–3 minutes, until softened. Season with salt, remove from the heat and keep warm.

Now cook the tuna. Mix the mushroom powder and Madras spice powder together on a large plate and roll the tuna logs in it until coated on all sides. Heat the vegetable oil in a large frying pan until it is very hot, then sear the tuna for 30–40 seconds on each side. Transfer the tuna to a warm plate and leave to rest for 2–3 minutes; it should still be raw in the centre.

To serve, place the squash in the centre of each plate and place a spoonful of mushrooms and spring onions on top. Cut each tuna log in half diagonally, place on the mushrooms and spring onions and season with salt. Place 4–6 pieces of pickled beetroot on each plate and drizzle some of the pickling juice around.

roasted prawns seasoned with tea and spice oil ~

MASALA CHAI KE JHINGAE

Chef Tetsuya Wakuda, of Tetsuya's restaurant in Sydney, Australia, is one of my heroes. This dish was inspired by one of his recipes, a witty take on the Indian spiced tea, *masala chai*, which happens to be my favourite drink for chilly winter days. Indians love their spices so much that they add them to their tea as well.

Alternative fish
smaller prawns, langoustines or even
  shrimps

SERVES 4

8–10 headless raw jumbo prawns
1 teaspoon Darjeeling tea, ground to
  a fine powder in a spice grinder
1 teaspoon crushed black
  peppercorns
vegetable oil for deep-frying
50g spinach leaves, cut into strips
1 tablespoon sherry vinegar
1 teaspoon chaat masala
sea salt
crisp, deep-fried spring onion strips,
  to garnish (optional)

For the spice oil
1 vanilla pod
3–4 green cardamom pods, crushed
1 teaspoon fennel seeds, lightly
  toasted in a dry frying pan and then
  crushed
½ teaspoon black peppercorns,
  crushed
a pinch of saffron strands
100ml vegetable oil

For the spice oil, slit the vanilla pod open lengthwise and scrape out the seeds with the point of a knife. Put them in a pan with all the remaining ingredients for the spice oil and heat to 80°C. Remove from the heat and leave to cool. (You won't need all the spice oil but it will keep in a sealed jar for 3–4 days.)

Peel the prawns and, using the point of a sharp knife, remove the dark, intestinal vein running down their backs. Cut them lengthwise in half, then season with the powdered tea, crushed black pepper and some salt. Put them on a baking tray, place in an oven preheated to 240°C/Gas Mark 9 and roast for 3–4 minutes or until they are just cooked through. Meanwhile, heat some oil in a deep-fat fryer or a deep saucepan, add the spinach and deep-fry for just a few seconds, until crisp. Remove and drain on kitchen paper.

Mix 2 tablespoons of the spice oil with the sherry vinegar. Place the deep-fried spinach in the centre of each plate and season with the chaat masala. Place the prawns on top, drizzle with the oil and vinegar mixture and then garnish with the spring onions, if using.

salmon poached in spice broth with pickled cucumber and duck egg emulsion ‒

BHAAP KI MACHCHI AUR KHEERAE KA SALAD

Poaching and steaming are not common cooking methods for fish in India, but there's no rule that would prohibit it being cooked in this way. I like playing with sweet and sour flavours, and poached fish is so simple in taste that it blends well with the tangy flavours of pickled cucumber.

Alternative fish
sea trout, rainbow trout, mackerel, lemon sole

SERVES 4

2 litres Fish Stock (see page 203)
1 teaspoon fennel seeds
½ teaspoon coriander seeds
1 carrot, sliced
1 onion, sliced
a small knob of fresh ginger, crushed
a small bunch of coriander leaves
4 x 150g pieces of salmon fillet, skinned
sprigs of dill, to garnish

For the pickled cucumber
150ml white wine vinegar
500ml water
1 tablespoon caster sugar
1 teaspoon salt
1 dried red chilli
1 teaspoon mustard seeds
1 teaspoon finely chopped fresh ginger
1 large cucumber, thinly sliced
1 tablespoon finely chopped dill

For the duck egg emulsion
2 duck egg yolks
1 tablespoon lemon juice
100g unsalted butter, melted
1 tablespoon finely chopped spring onions
¼ teaspoon red chilli flakes
sea salt

First prepare the pickled cucumber. Put the vinegar, water, sugar, salt, dried chilli, mustard seeds and ginger in a pan and bring to the boil. Add the cucumber, then remove from the heat and leave to cool. Stir in the chopped dill and store in the fridge.

For the duck egg emulsion, beat the egg yolks together in a bowl, then set the bowl over a pan of simmering water, making sure the water does not touch the base of the bowl. Continue to beat with a handheld electric mixer or a whisk until the yolks start to thicken, then gradually beat in the lemon juice. Beat in the melted butter a teaspoon at a time until you have a thick, glossy emulsion. Add the spring onions and chilli flakes and season to taste with salt. Keep warm while you cook the fish.

Bring the fish stock to the boil in a large pan and add the fennel seeds, coriander seeds, carrot, onion, ginger and coriander leaves. Reduce to a simmer, lower the pieces of salmon into the stock and poach very gently for 3–4 minutes, until the fish feels firm. Remove from the poaching liquor with a fish slice.

Divide the pickled cucumber between 4 plates, top with the fish and then spoon the duck egg emulsion on top. Garnish with sprigs of dill and serve immediately.

ROASTED MONKFISH WITH chutNey pressed Rice

PEIXE CAFREAL

Cafreal, a spicy chicken dish, was brought to India from Africa by the Portuguese. It has been part of the Goan cooking repertoire for more than 450 years now and works very well with meaty fish such as monkfish. I have combined this recipe with *poha*, a Hindu pressed rice dish. Pressed rice flakes are made by parboiling the rice and then pressing the grains flat with a mechanical press, or by pounding and sun-drying them. They are widely available in Asian supermarkets, or you can order them online through www.spicesofindia.co.uk.

Alternative fish
swordfish, turbot, halibut

SERVES 4

4 x 150g pieces of thick monkfish tail
aged balsamic vinegar, for drizzling
sea salt
amaranth cress, to garnish (optional)

For the cafreal masala
1 tablespoon coriander seeds
1 teaspoon cumin seeds
3 cloves
4 green cardamom pods
6–7 black peppercorns
2.5cm piece of cinnamon stick
a small blade of mace
1 star anise
1 tablespoon chopped fresh ginger
3–4 garlic cloves
2 Dutch green chillies
a small bunch of coriander leaves
3 tablespoons white wine vinegar
4 tablespoons vegetable oil

For the poha
150g poha rice (pressed rice flakes)
2 tablespoons vegetable oil
1 teaspoon mustard seeds
5–6 curry leaves
1 green chilli, slit open lengthwise
1 onion, finely chopped
1 potato, boiled until tender, then
   peeled and diced
4 tablespoons peanuts, skinned
½ teaspoon ground turmeric
1 tablespoon lime juice
1 tablespoon finely chopped
   coriander leaves
2–3 tablespoons Spicy Tomato
   Chutney (see page 206)
sea salt

For the cafreal masala, toast the coriander, cumin, cloves, cardamom, peppercorns, cinnamon, mace and star anise in a dry frying pan until aromatic, then put them in a blender or food processor with the remaining masala ingredients. Blend to a paste and season with salt. Apply this paste liberally to the monkfish and leave in the fridge for 1 hour.

Put the fish on a lightly greased baking tray, place in an oven preheated to 220°C/Gas Mark 7 and cook for 7–9 minutes, until just done. Remove from the oven and leave to rest for 2–3 minutes.

For the poha, wash the pressed rice in cold running water, then leave to soak in a bowl of water. Meanwhile, heat the oil in a saucepan, add the mustard seeds, curry leaves and green chilli and sauté until the seeds start to pop. Immediately add the onion and sauté until translucent. Add the diced potato, peanuts and turmeric and sauté for 2–3 minutes. Drain the rice and stir it into the pan. Cook over a medium heat for 3–4 minutes, then remove from the heat and add the lime juice, chopped coriander and some salt. Stir in the tomato chutney to bring all the ingredients together.

To serve, place the poha mixture slightly off centre on each plate. Slice the monkfish and lean it on the poha, then drizzle with balsamic vinegar. Garnish with the amaranth cress, if using.

'Barramundi's flavour
comes alive with spices.
The fish has got so much flavour
that it needs strong tastes
to work with.'

SPICE-ROASTED BARRAMUNDI, PAGE 140.

STEAMED SEA TROUT WITH SPICE SALT AND pickled fennel —

The arrival of sea trout on the fishmonger's slab is a sign that summer will soon be here. I like to team it with delicate flavours. Here it is coated in a light marinade, then steamed and served with pickled fennel and spice salt. None of the ingredients overpowers the flavour of the fish itself.

Alternative fish
salmon, trout, mackerel, lemon sole

SERVES 4

2 tablespoons plain yoghurt
1 teaspoon lime juice
1 teaspoon crushed black
   peppercorns
4 x 150g pieces of sea trout fillet, pin
   bones removed
4 sprigs of chervil, to garnish

For the pickled fennel
2 fennel bulbs, thinly sliced
1 teaspoon fennel seeds
¼ teaspoon ground turmeric
70ml white vinegar or white wine
   vinegar
30g caster sugar
a few chervil leaves
sea salt

For the spice salt
2 teaspoons vegetable oil
1 teaspoon fenugreek seeds
1 teaspoon coriander seeds
1 teaspoon cumin seeds
½ teaspoon red chilli flakes
1 teaspoon sea salt
1 teaspoon finely chopped dill

First prepare the pickled fennel. Put all the ingredients except the chervil in a heavy-based pan, bring to a simmer and cook for 4–5 minutes, until the fennel has softened. Remove from the heat and leave to marinate in the liquid in the fridge overnight.

For the spice salt, lightly smear a small frying pan with the oil and sauté all the spices (but not the salt and dill leaves) one by one, until they darken slightly. Transfer them to a mortar and pestle and pound to a coarse mixture. At this stage, the spice mixture can be stored in an airtight container for 3–4 days. Mix together the yoghurt, lime juice and crushed pepper and spread them over the fish. Leave to marinate for 15–20 minutes. Wrap each piece of fish in cling film, place in a steamer and steam for 3–5 minutes, depending on the thickness of the fillet. Unwrap the fish and remove the skin, if you prefer. Mix the salt and chopped dill with the spice mixture and sprinkle it liberally on the skin side of the fish.

To serve, mix the pickled fennel with the chervil leaves. Spoon it in the centre of each plate and place the spiced fish on top. Drizzle some of the fennel marinade around the plate and garnish with a chervil sprig.

tamilian cinnamon-smoked river fish ⟶

LULA BEDUMA

Cinnamon is the dominant flavour in this dish. Lula are dark-coloured freshwater fish. In this country-style recipe, the fillets are traditionally tinted with red and yellow pigments from the bark of the gammalu and jackfruit trees. The bark is soaked overnight and then the liquid is boiled to intensify the colour. To get a similar effect, I use salmon or sea trout in the UK and smoke it lightly.

Alternative fish
rainbow trout, Arctic char

SERVES 6–8

1kg salmon or sea trout, filleted
2 star fruit, sliced

For the marinade
250g star fruit, crushed in a food
　processor
100g rock salt
1½ teaspoons honey
10 basil leaves
1 teaspoon Garlic Paste (see page 202)
½ teaspoon ground turmeric
1 teaspoon red chilli powder
2 tablespoons lemon juice
2 tablespoons vegetable oil
4 cloves, pounded to a powder
4 cardamom pods, pounded to a
　powder
¼ teaspoon ground cinnamon

For smoking the fish
10 large cinnamon sticks
4 cloves
2–3 drops of cinnamon oil (available
　from healthfood shops)

For the badum (sauce)
50ml vegetable oil
10–12 curry leaves
2 red onions, sliced
10g pandanus leaves (rampe)
500ml coconut milk

Cut the fish fillets into 7cm pieces. Mix all the marinade ingredients together to make a paste and spread it on the fillets. Leave to marinate in the fridge for 8–10 hours.

For smoking, heat a wok over a low heat. Add the cinnamon sticks, cloves and cinnamon oil. When it begins to smoke, place the fish fillets on a rack at least 2cm above the smoking ingredients. Cover with foil and smoke for 10–15 minutes; when the fish is ready, it will look slightly darker and the flavour of the smoke will have penetrated the flesh.

To prepare the sauce, heat the oil in a pan, add the curry leaves and sauté for a minute. Add the onions and sauté until browned. Add the pandanus leaves and coconut milk, bring to a simmer and cook for 2–3 minutes, to let the flavours infuse. Add the smoked fish fillets and cook for 3–5 minutes, until the flesh firms up. Serve straight away, garnished with the star fruit slices and accompanied by boiled rice.

FISH – INDIAN STYLE

grilled jumbo prawns in a chilli-garlic marinade with noodle salad

CHENGRI NOODLE

This was inspired by the Chinese food of Kolkata (formerly Calcutta). The prawns are marinated Indian style and grilled or barbecued, but the accompanying noodle salad is utterly Chinese in character – it works!

Alternative fish
smaller prawns, mussels, crab, lobster, crayfish, any white fish

SERVES 4

8 raw jumbo prawns
lime wedges, to serve

For the chilli-garlic marinade
1½ teaspoons Garlic Paste
  (see page 202)
1 small green chilli, finely chopped
1 tablespoon tomato paste
½ teaspoon crushed coriander seeds
1 teaspoon finely chopped fresh ginger
1 tablespoon vegetable oil
½ teaspoon chaat masala
1 tablespoon lemon juice
1 teaspoon finely grated lemon zest
½ teaspoon palm sugar or brown
  sugar
sea salt

For the dressing
2 tablespoons finely chopped fresh
  ginger
1 tablespoon sesame oil
3 tablespoons red wine vinegar
1 tablespoon Spicy Indian Ketchup
  (see page 209)
1 garlic clove, crushed
a pinch of sugar
soy sauce (optional)

For the noodle salad
250g instant noodles
5 spring onions, sliced on the diagonal
2 tablespoons chopped coriander leaves
1 red pepper, cut into fine strips
100g snow peas (mangetout), cut in half

Peel the prawns, leaving the head and tail shell on. Using the tip of a sharp knife, remove the dark intestinal vein running down their backs. Mix together all the ingredients for the marinade. Coat the prawns in the marinade and set aside for about 5 minutes.

Mix all the ingredients for the dressing together and set aside until required.

Cook the prawns under a preheated grill or on a barbecue for 3–5 minutes on each side (if you are using smaller prawns, reduce the time to 2–3 minutes per side).

For the salad, cook the noodles in plenty of boiling water for 2 minutes (or according to the packet instructions), then drain and refresh in cold water. Mix them with the spring onions, coriander, red pepper and snow peas, then toss with the dressing. Serve the grilled prawns with the salad and some lime wedges.

chickpea flour cannelloni of spicy prawns with tomato-pepper sauce ~

JHINGAE KE CHILAY

We came up with a vegetarian version of this innovative dish for the menu at Benares but I often change it to seafood.

Alternative fish shrimps

SERVES 4

vegetable oil for deep-frying
500g small peeled raw prawns
2 onions, finely chopped
5–6 curry leaves
1 large tomato, chopped
1 teaspoon brown sugar
sea salt
coriander and celery cress (or sprigs of coriander), to garnish

For the spice paste
2 teaspoons red chilli flakes
5cm piece of cinnamon stick
6–7 green cardamom pods
6–7 cloves
½ teaspoon ground black pepper
½ teaspoon cumin seeds
1 tablespoon Ginger-Garlic Paste (see page 202)
1 tablespoon finely chopped fresh ginger
100ml white wine vinegar or malt vinegar

For the tomato-pepper sauce
2 tablespoons vegetable oil
1 teaspoon chopped garlic
½ teaspoon cumin seeds
1 onion, sliced
3 tomatoes, chopped
½ teaspoon ground coriander
¼ teaspoon red chilli powder
½ teaspoon garam masala
1 red pepper, roasted, peeled and chopped
1 tablespoon finely chopped coriander leaves

For the chickpea flour pancakes
200g gram (chickpea) flour
1 tablespoon cornflour
1 green chilli, finely chopped
1 onion, finely chopped
1 teaspoon finely chopped fresh ginger
1 tablespoon chopped coriander leaves
1 tablespoon vegetable oil, plus a little extra for frying
150ml plain or carbonated water

Put all the ingredients for the spice paste in a blender or food processor and blend until smooth, then set aside.

Heat the oil for deep-frying in a wok, add the prawns and fry for 2 minutes. Remove with a slotted spoon and leave on kitchen paper to drain.

Heat 3 tablespoons of the oil in a separate pan, add the onions and cook over a medium heat until golden brown. Add the curry leaves and spice paste and cook for 2 minutes, then add the chopped tomato and cook for 3–5 minutes, until the tomato blends with the rest of the ingredients. Add the prawns, followed by the sugar and some salt, then cook, stirring, for 2–3 minutes. Remove from the heat and keep warm. (You could make the prawn mixture in advance and store it in a sealed container in the fridge for 6–8 days.)

Next make the tomato-pepper sauce. Heat the oil in a pan, add the garlic and cumin seeds and sauté until the seeds start to pop. Add the onion and sauté until translucent. Stir in the tomatoes and ground spices and cook over a medium heat for 5–7 minutes. Add the roasted pepper, then season with salt to taste. Stir in the coriander leaves, remove from the heat and keep warm.

For the pancakes, whisk all the ingredients together in a bowl with a pinch of salt. Heat a little oil in a non-stick frying pan and pour in a small ladleful of batter. Tilt the pan quickly to spread the batter evenly over the surface, then cook over a medium heat for 1–2 minutes, until lightly coloured underneath. Flip the pancake over and cook on the other side for 1–2 minutes. Transfer to a well-oiled baking tray and repeat with the remaining batter to make 8 pancakes.

To assemble, place a pancake flat on a board and put about 1½ tablespoons of the warm prawn mixture in the centre. Roll it up tightly, then trim off the sides and cut it into 5cm cylinders. Repeat with the remaining pancakes.

Spoon the tomato-pepper sauce into the centre of each plate and place 2 cylinders on top. Garnish with cress or coriander sprigs and serve straight away.

whole salmon baked in a foil parcel with rose petals ~

DUM KI AKKHI MACHCHI

This is based on a very old cooking method from Lucknow, where the fish is sealed in an earthenware pot and cooked in a coal-fired pit for about 6 hours. I don't have the patience to wait that long – hence this very effective shortcut.

SERVES 6–8

1 x 1.5kg salmon, scaled and cleaned
2 tablespoons lemon juice
1 tablespoon Ginger-Garlic Paste
  (see page 202)
1 teaspoon red chilli powder
50g blanched pistachio nuts
2 teaspoons ground fennel seeds
½ teaspoon ground star anise
1 teaspoon ground caraway seeds
400g thick yoghurt
50g melted butter
sea salt

For the gram flour roux
1 tablespoon vegetable oil
2 tablespoons gram flour, lightly
  toasted in a dry frying pan

For the rose paste
15 blanched almonds
25g desiccated coconut
1 tablespoon pine nuts
1 tablespoon dried rose petals
  (available from Mediterranean
  grocer's shops or healthfood shops)
1 teaspoon rosewater
2 tablespoons poppy seeds, soaked in
  warm water for 2 hours

For the spice paste
2 blades of mace
3 green cardamom pods
1 black cardamom pod
5 cloves
1 teaspoon black peppercorns

Sprinkle the salmon inside and out with the lemon juice and some salt, then set aside.

To make the roux, heat the oil in a small, heavy-based pan, add the flour and cook, stirring, over a medium heat for 3–4 minutes, until it forms a thick paste. Remove from the heat and leave to cool.

Put all the ingredients for the rose paste in a small food processor and whiz to a paste, adding a little water. Remove from the food processor and set aside. Put all the ingredients for the spice paste in the processor with a little water and process to a paste.

In a bowl, mix the rose paste, spice paste, ginger-garlic paste, chilli powder, pistachios, fennel, star anise, caraway, gram flour roux and yoghurt together. Grease a large sheet of foil, put it on a greased baking sheet and place the salmon in the centre. Carefully put the stuffing in the cavity, then pour the melted butter over the fish. Bring the ends of the foil up over the salmon to make a loose parcel and then pinch and fold them a few times until well sealed. Place in an oven preheated to 220°C/Gas Mark 7 and bake for 30 minutes.

Remove the fish from the oven and open the parcel. Peel off the skin from the top of the salmon with a small, sharp knife, then turn the fish over and repeat on the other side. Cut into portions and serve with the stuffing.

CRAB and guava salad with tangerine and mustard dressing

KEKDAE AUR AMROOD KA SALAD

I like to create dishes by combining ingredients that are local to each other. In Goa I found crab and guava went naturally together – add local oranges or passion fruit to make a dressing and you have a winning recipe. This light, perky salad gives you perfectly balanced flavours on a hot summer's day.

SERVES 4

1 tablespoon vegetable oil
¼ teaspoon red chilli flakes or crushed black peppercorns
¼ teaspoon coriander seeds, lightly toasted in a dry frying pan and then crushed
a pinch of ground cloves
¼ teaspoon ground turmeric
300g fresh white crab meat, flaked
1 tablespoon desiccated coconut, lightly toasted in a dry frying pan
2 tablespoons coconut milk
1 teaspoon lime juice
1 tablespoon chopped coriander leaves
a few coriander sprigs
½ red pepper, cut into fine strips
2 ripe guavas, peeled, deseeded and cut into wedges
sea salt

For the tangerine and mustard dressing
70ml tangerine juice
1½ teaspoons Tamarind Pulp (see page 218)
1 tablespoon coconut oil or vegetable oil
1 teaspoon wholegrain mustard
2 teaspoons palm sugar
½ teaspoon cumin seeds, lightly toasted in a dry frying pan and then crushed
1 tablespoon finely chopped fresh ginger

Mix all the ingredients for the dressing together and set aside until required.

For the salad, heat the oil in a pan, add the red chilli flakes, coriander seeds, ground cloves and turmeric and sauté for 1 minute. Stir in the flaked crab meat and toasted desiccated coconut and sauté for a minute, then add the coconut milk and lime juice. Remove from the heat and leave to cool.

Put the crab meat mixture, chopped coriander, coriander sprigs, red pepper and guava wedges into a large bowl. Add three-quarters of the dressing, toss the salad well, then taste and add salt if necessary (crab is naturally salty, so you may not need any). Drizzle the remaining dressing over the top and serve straight away.

from friends & family ~

Avijit gosh's spicy fish curry ~

MACHER JHAL

I shared a flat with Avijit when I was training at the Oberoi School in New Delhi. He has gone on to become a great pastry chef but, since he is a Bengali, his passion for fish is still alive and swimming. This recipe is from our student days – when he rarely used to cook for me.

Alternative fish
cod, sea bass, snapper

SERVES 4

4 x 125g pieces of carp fillet, skinned and cut in half
2 tablespoons vegetable oil
½ teaspoon Panch Phoran (see page 217)
1 onion, finely sliced
½ teaspoon ground turmeric
½ teaspoon red chilli powder
3 tablespoons white mustard seeds, soaked in cold water for 3–4 hours and then ground to a paste (or use 1 tablespoon English mustard)
1 tablespoon poppy seeds, soaked in ½ cup of water for 3–4 hours, then drained and ground to a paste
250ml water
1 tomato, cut into quarters
2 green chillies, slit open lengthwise
½ teaspoon caster sugar
sea salt

Season the fish with salt. Heat half the oil in a large, non-stick frying pan, add the fish and fry for 2 minutes on each side, until light golden. Remove from the pan and keep warm.

Heat the remaining oil in the pan, then add the panch phoran and cook for a minute or two, until it splutters. Add the onion and sauté until golden. Add the turmeric, red chilli powder and some salt, then add the mustard and poppy seed pastes and stir well. Add the water a little at a time and continue to simmer on a low heat for 4–5 minutes (take care not to let the mixture boil or it could turn bitter). Slip in the fried fish, tomato quarters and slit green chillies and simmer for 2–3 minutes, until the sauce coats the fish. Finish with the sugar, then remove from the heat and serve with boiled rice.

jitin johi's dover sole with prawn pickle ~

Jitin is executive chef at Vatika, my restaurant at Wykeham Vineyard in Hampshire. An intelligent and gifted cook, he is enjoying his freedom there after several years at Benares. I love his simple treatment for Dover sole.

Alternative fish
lemon sole, plaice

SERVES 4

4 small Dover sole, cleaned
plain flour for dusting
2–3 tablespoons vegetable oil
sea salt

For the prawn pickle
1 tablespoon mustard oil or vegetable oil
1 teaspoon Panch Phoran (see page 217)
3 red onions, chopped
12 curry leaves
1 tablespoon tomato paste
100g small peeled prawns
2 tablespoons mayonnaise
juice of 1 lime
a bunch of dill, chopped

For the marinade
1½ teaspoons ground turmeric
1 teaspoon ajwain seeds
2 tablespoons Ginger-Garlic Paste
(see page 202)

To make the prawn pickle, heat the oil in a small pan, add the panch phoran and cook over a medium heat until it crackles. Add the onions and sauté for 1–2 minutes, then add the curry leaves, tomato paste and some salt and cook over a low heat for 5–7 minutes, until the onions are soft. Add the prawns and cook for 2–3 minutes, then remove from the heat and leave to cool. Stir in the mayonnaise, lime juice and dill and store in the fridge.

Mix together all the ingredients for the marinade and add a pinch of salt. Rub the marinade over the fish and set aside for 10–12 minutes.

Dust the fish with flour. Heat the oil in a large frying pan, add the fish and fry over a medium heat for 2–3 minutes on each side. Serve accompanied by the pickle.

FISH — INDIAN STYLE

jitin's steamed salmon trout with bok choy and ginger

This recipe from Jitin is easy and fuss free. I have cooked it several times now and it's a real winner.

Alternative fish
salmon, halibut, turbot

SERVES 4

3 tablespoons soy sauce
2 tablespoons oyster sauce
2 teaspoons sesame oil
2.5cm piece of fresh ginger, cut into fine shreds
2 heads of bok choy, trimmed and shredded
2 garlic cloves, chopped
4 x 125g pieces of salmon trout fillet
120g sushi rice
8 tablespoons caster sugar
8 tablespoons rice vinegar

Mix together the soy sauce, oyster sauce, sesame oil, ginger, bok choy and garlic. Place the fish fillets in a steamer, spread the bok choy mixture on top and steam for 5–6 minutes, until the fish is just done.

Measure the rice in a jug and then put it in a pan. Measure out double the amount of water and add to the pan. Bring to the boil, cover and simmer until the rice is cooked and the water has been absorbed.

Put the sugar and vinegar in a small pan and bring to the boil, stirring to dissolve the sugar. Pour it over the cooked rice. Serve the fish accompanied by the rice.

NAVEEN BHATIA'S TILAPIA IN *yoghurt* AND MUSTARD SAUCE —

DAHI SARSON MACCH

Naveen was my teacher at the Oberoi and is now a good friend. After landing me my first job in the UK, he followed me here a few years later. His teachings have had a huge influence on my cooking – he is undoubtedly one of my food heroes.

Alternative fish
any firm-fleshed fish, such as swordfish, monkfish or kingfish

SERVES 4

½ teaspoon red chilli powder
¼ teaspoon ground turmeric
4 x 150g tilapia fillets, skinned
3 tablespoons vegetable oil
½ teaspoon mustard seeds
10 curry leaves
2 onions, chopped
1 teaspoon finely chopped fresh
  ginger
1 green chilli, deseeded and sliced
2 tomatoes, chopped
1 teaspoon ground coriander
4 green cardamom pods
8 tablespoons thick yoghurt, lightly
  whisked
2 teaspoons chopped coriander
  leaves, plus a few whole leaves to
  garnish
sea salt

Mix together the red chilli powder, half the turmeric and some salt and rub them over the fish fillets. Set aside for 5 minutes.

Heat the oil in a large, heavy-based frying pan, add the fillets and fry for just 1 minute per side; do not cook them fully. Remove from the pan and place on kitchen paper to drain.

Heat a little more oil in the pan, if necessary, and add the mustard seeds. When they start to crackle, add the curry leaves and chopped onions and sauté until the onions are translucent. Stir in the ginger, green chilli, tomatoes, ground coriander, the remaining turmeric and the cardamom pods and cook until the tomatoes are soft. Add the yoghurt and bring to a simmer over a low heat. Add the fried tilapia and cook for just a minute, then sprinkle with the chopped coriander and adjust the seasoning. Serve immediately, garnished with coriander leaves and accompanied by some steamed basmati rice and stir-fried green beans.

FISH – INDIAN STYLE

BALAJI'S BALACHENDER'S SOUTH INDIAN fiSH SANdWICH

VAVA MEEN ROAST

This recipe has been provided by Bala, my head chef at Benares and a talented, versatile cook. Bala comes from Chennai (Madras), so his sense of spicing is quite different from that of North Indian cooks – I guess that's what makes him so special in my kitchen.

Alternative fish
any flat fish

SERVES 4

½ teaspoon red chilli powder
1 teaspoon ground coriander
½ teaspoon ground turmeric
2 tablespoons Tamarind Pulp
  (see page 218)
4 small plaice, filleted
sea salt

For the crab mixture
5–6 tablespoons vegetable oil
1 teaspoon cumin seeds
2 green cardamom pods
1 bay leaf
2.5cm piece of cinnamon stick
3 cloves
5 black peppercorns
2 onions, chopped
25g Ginger-Garlic Paste (see page 202)
3 tomatoes, chopped
¼ teaspoon ground turmeric
1½ teaspoons ground coriander
½ teaspoon red chilli powder
250g fresh white crab meat
1 tablespoon finely chopped
  coriander leaves

Mix together the chilli powder, coriander, turmeric, tamarind and some salt and use to coat the plaice fillets. Set aside to marinate while you prepare the crab mixture.

Heat 4 tablespoons of the vegetable oil in a pan, add the whole spices and sauté until they crackle. Add the onions, sauté until light brown, then stir in the ginger-garlic paste and sauté for 2–3 minutes. Add the tomatoes, turmeric, coriander and chilli powder and sauté for 8–10 minutes, until the tomatoes have turned into a thick sauce. Stir in the crab meat, season with salt if necessary, and then sprinkle with the chopped coriander.

Put the plaice fillets on a baking tray and place under a hot grill, flesh-side up. Cook for 1–2 minutes, until the flesh firms up a little. Sandwich the fillets together with the crab mixture, making sure the skin is on the outside. Return to the grill for 3–5 minutes, turning once, until the fish is completely cooked. Serve immediately.

bala's *fried fish* —

CHAPA VEPUDU

This is a popular snack on the streets and beaches of India. Bala fries the fish but you could grill it instead, if you prefer. I have reduced the scary amount of red chilli in the original recipe and substituted tomato paste instead. If you are feeling brave, replace the tomato paste with red chilli paste!

Alternative fish
mackerel, bream, salmon, John Dory

SERVES 4

500g kingfish, cut into 8 steaks
cornflour for dusting
vegetable oil for shallow-frying
lemon wedges, to serve

For the paste
1 teaspoon red chilli powder
2 tablespoons tomato paste
1 tablespoon Ginger-Garlic Paste (see page 202)
1 tablespoon gram flour
juice of 2 limes
sea salt

Mix together all the ingredients for the paste. Coat the fish steaks with the paste and leave to marinate for 15–20 minutes.

Dust the fish lightly with cornflour. Heat a thin layer of vegetable oil in a large frying pan, add the fish and cook for about 5 minutes, turning frequently. Serve with the lemon wedges.

jUN TaNaKa's MacKereL fONDant WITH pickLeD veGeTaBLes ~

Jun is a remarkably talented chef, who I met on the set of the BBC television series, *Food Poker*. I love this recipe so much that I told him if he didn't contribute it to the book I would be forced to steal it. Fortunately he was happy to let me have it. It's simple to make, but a good way to impress your friends with your culinary talent.

SERVES 4 AS A STARTER

2 x 300g mackerel, filleted
a little melted butter for brushing
1 shallot, chopped
1 carrot, chopped
1 garlic clove, sliced
a sprig of thyme
a sprig of tarragon
juice of ½ lemon
50ml white wine
½ bunch of chives
1 tablespoon creamed horseradish
sea salt and freshly ground black pepper
coriander cress (or sprigs of coriander), to garnish

For the pickled vegetables
150ml olive oil
200g button onions, peeled
2 globe artichokes, outer leaves and choke removed, then trimmed and cut into wedges
200g cauliflower florets
½ bunch of baby carrots, peeled and cut in half
1 teaspoon coriander seeds
a sprig of thyme
1 garlic clove, crushed
a pinch of saffron strands, infused in 150ml warm water
100ml white wine vinegar

First prepare the pickled vegetables. Heat the olive oil in a pan, add the button onions and cook for 3 minutes. Add the globe artichokes and cook for a further 3 minutes, then add the cauliflower, carrots, coriander seeds, thyme, garlic and some salt. Cook for 2 minutes, then pour in the saffron water and the vinegar and bring to the boil. Cook at a gentle simmer for 15 minutes, until the vegetables are just tender. Remove from the heat and keep warm.

To prepare the mackerel, cut the fillets lengthwise in half and remove the pin bones. Take 4 metal rings, 4cm high and 5cm in diameter, brush with melted butter and place on a baking tray. Cut the mackerel into batons the same height as the rings. Season with salt and pepper and line the rings with the mackerel, skin-side facing outwards and alternating between black and white skin. When the rings are lined, cut the skin off the remaining mackerel fillet and use to fill the centre of the rings.

Scatter the shallot, carrot, garlic, thyme and tarragon around the fondants and pour the lemon juice and wine into the tray. Cover the tray with cling film and cook in an oven preheated to 100°C (or the lowest possible gas setting) for 10–12 minutes, until the mackerel has firmed up.

Remove the baking tray from the oven. Mix the chives with the horseradish and use to coat the top of the fondants. Place one in the centre of each serving plate, arrange the pickled vegetables around and then take off the rings. Garnish with coriander and serve.

sriram kailasam's fried grouper with sweet chilli sauce —

Sriram is another friend from student days. He was a naughty one, but very bright. Based in Bangkok, he is in charge of the food and beverage department of Banyan Tree Hotels and Resorts Worldwide, and consequently there is a strong Thai influence in his food – exemplified by dishes such as this one.

Alternative fish
sea bass, turbot, red snapper

SERVES 4

2 tablespoons Thai fish sauce
¼ teaspoon ground white pepper
4 x 150g grouper fillets
vegetable oil for deep-frying
10 sprigs of Thai sweet basil,
   deep-fried, to garnish (optional)

For the sweet chilli sauce
1 tablespoon vegetable oil
2 garlic cloves, finely chopped
1 onion, finely chopped
2 large red chillies, finely chopped
4 red bird's eye chillies, finely
   chopped
100g fresh pineapple, cut into 1cm dice
2 tomatoes, skinned and cut into
   1cm dice
4 tablespoons brown sugar
100ml water
1 teaspoon salt
4 tablespoons rice wine vinegar or
   white wine vinegar
1 tablespoon cornflour, mixed to a
   paste with 2 tablespoons water

For the sauce, heat the vegetable oil in a pan, add the garlic, onion and chillies and fry for 5 minutes, until softened. Add the pineapple and tomatoes and fry for 2 minutes longer. Add the sugar, water, salt and vinegar and bring to the boil. Simmer for 10 minutes, then add the cornflour paste and bring back to the boil, stirring. Remove from the heat and leave to cool.

Sprinkle the fish sauce and white pepper over the grouper fillets and leave to marinate for 10 minutes. Heat the oil in a large frying pan, add the fish, skin-side down, and fry for 2–3 minutes, until the skin is golden and crisp. Turn and fry for another couple of minutes, until the fish is cooked through. Reheat the sweet chilli sauce and serve with the fish, garnished with fried basil, if liked.

sriram's curried fish soufflés

This makes a good starter, or could be served as the fish course in a formal dinner. Sriram's food has always been witty, and this soufflé with a twist is a great example.

Alternative fish
salmon, sea trout, sea bass

SERVES 4

500g grouper fillet, skinned
5 tablespoons red curry paste
2 teaspoons finely chopped fresh
  ginger
2 eggs
300ml coconut milk, plus a little extra
  to serve
4 kaffir lime leaves, finely sliced
2 tablespoons Thai fish sauce
2 teaspoons caster sugar
8 basil leaves
a little finely sliced red chilli, to
  garnish

Put 300g of the grouper fillet in a food processor and pulse until minced. Transfer to a bowl, add the curry paste, ginger and eggs and mix well. Stir in the coconut milk, kaffir lime leaves, fish sauce and sugar.

Cut the remaining grouper fillet into 16 equal pieces. Put the basil leaves in 4 ramekin dishes and put half the curry mixture on top. Add the pieces of grouper and top with the remaining curry mixture. Put the dishes in a steamer and steam for 15 minutes, until the soufflés have firmed up. Drizzle over a little coconut milk, garnish with sliced red chilli and serve immediately.

FISH – INDIAN STYLE

DEEPTI'S *fish* AND *kale* TART

My wife, Deepti, is a creative cook. It's not me she finds a challenge to cook for but the children. She plans her cooking well in advance and that keeps them interested. We all love this recipe of hers. She doesn't mind using ready-made pastry cases but I have included the pastry recipe for purists. You could use smoked fish in this tart but I prefer plain fish because of the spices.

SERVES 6

400g salmon trout or salmon fillet
a few sprigs of coriander
1 bay leaf
½ teaspoon black peppercorns
about 1 litre whole milk
1 tablespoon vegetable oil
50g unsalted butter
1 teaspoon finely chopped garlic
½ teaspoon red chilli flakes
½ teaspoon coriander seeds
2 onions, finely sliced
300g kale, shredded
1 teaspoon ground coriander
½ teaspoon ground turmeric
½ teaspoon garam masala
50g sun-dried tomatoes, chopped
200ml double cream
2 eggs
2 egg yolks
50g mature Cheddar cheese, grated
sea salt and freshly ground black pepper

For the pastry
150g plain white flour
50g fine semolina
a pinch of salt
100g chilled unsalted butter, cubed
1 egg, separated
50ml milk

Make the pastry first. Put the flour, semolina, salt and butter into a food processor and pulse until the mixture resembles breadcrumbs. Add the egg yolk and then, with the processor running, slowly add the milk, stopping as soon as the ingredients come together into a dough; you may not need all the milk. Tip out on to a floured surface and knead lightly for a minute to make a smooth ball. Wrap in cling film and chill for 30 minutes. Roll the pastry out thinly on lightly floured surface and then use to line a 25cm loose-bottomed tart tin. Leave a little excess pastry overhanging the sides of the tin, as it will shrink during cooking. Prick the base of the pastry case with a fork, then cover the base and sides with baking parchment and fill with baking beans. Place the tart on a baking sheet in an oven preheated to 180°C/Gas Mark 4 and bake for 12–15 minutes, until beginning to colour lightly. Remove the beans and paper and return the pastry case to the oven for a few more minutes, until it is dry and cooked. To seal the pastry, lightly beat the egg white and brush it all over the pastry case. Return it to the oven for 3–4 minutes, until light golden. Trim off the excess pastry using a sharp knife.

Put the fish in a pan large enough to hold it in a single layer and add the coriander sprigs, bay leaf and peppercorns. Pour in enough milk just to cover the fish, then bring to a simmer and remove from the heat. The fish should be just cooked; if it isn't, leave it in the hot milk for a few minutes longer. Remove the fish from the pan, strain the milk and leave to cool.

Heat the oil and butter in a frying pan, add the garlic, chilli flakes and coriander seeds and sauté over a medium heat for 3–4 minutes, until the spices splutter and the garlic turns light brown. Add the onions and sauté until light brown. Drop in the kale shreds and cook for 5–6 minutes, until wilted, then raise the heat a little and cook for a further 3–4 minutes, until all the liquid released from the kale has evaporated. Stir in the ground spices and add salt to taste. Remove from the heat.

Flake the fish into a bowl, discarding the skin and bones. Add the kale mixture and the sun-dried tomatoes. Mix well and transfer to the pastry case. Beat 200ml of the strained fish poaching milk with the cream, eggs and egg yolks, then stir in the cheese. Season with salt and pepper and pour into the tart case. Bake at 180°C/Gas Mark 4 for 30 minutes, until lightly set and browned. Serve warm or cold.

OUR *family fish pie* ~

This recipe is for my daughter, Amisha. When her head teacher complained that she would not eat pies at school, Amisha told me that she didn't think they were very interesting. So I came up with this spicy version and shared the recipe with the dinner lady at her school. Amisha loves this pie. I cover it with shortcrust pastry but you could use puff pastry or mashed potato instead.

Alternative fish
coley, pollack, ling

SERVES 4

2 tablespoons vegetable or sunflower oil
1 onion, finely chopped
5–6 curry leaves
1 teaspoon finely chopped fresh ginger
1 carrot, cut into small dice and parboiled
2 potatoes, peeled, cut into small dice and parboiled
½ teaspoon ground turmeric
½ teaspoon garam masala
650ml coconut milk
300g farmed Shetland cod fillet, skinned and cut into cubes
300g undyed smoked haddock, skinned and cut into cubes
200g small prawns, peeled
1 courgette, cut into small dice
2 tomatoes, deseeded and chopped
2 tablespoons chopped coriander leaves
sea salt

For the pastry
200g plain white flour
a pinch of sea salt
100g chilled unsalted butter, cut into cubes
1 egg, separated
50ml milk

Make the pastry first. Put the flour, salt and butter into a food processor and pulse until the mixture resembles breadcrumbs. Add the egg yolk and then, with the processor running, slowly add the milk, stopping as soon as the ingredients come together into a dough; you may not need all the milk. Tip out on to a floured surface and knead lightly for a minute to make a smooth ball. Wrap in cling film and chill for 30 minutes.

Heat the oil in a large pan, add the onion and curry leaves and sauté for 3–5 minutes, until the onion is translucent. Add the ginger, diced carrot and potatoes and cook gently, without colouring, for 5–7 minutes, until the vegetables are almost cooked. Add the ground spices and some salt and sauté for 1–2 minutes, then pour in the coconut milk and bring to a simmer. Add the fish, prawns, courgette and tomatoes and cook for 3–5 minutes over a medium heat, stirring occasionally, until the fish is just done. Stir in the coriander leaves, adjust the seasoning and remove from the heat. Spoon the mixture into a large pie dish.

Roll the pastry out thinly on a lightly floured surface. Lift it up on the rolling pin and place it on top of the pie dish. Trim off the excess pastry, leaving 2.5cm extra on all sides. Lightly beat the egg white with a fork, then brush the sides of the dish with it and press the pastry on to it to seal. Brush the egg white on top of the pastry as well and then bake in an oven preheated to 200°C/Gas Mark 6 for 15–20 minutes, until the pastry is crisp and light golden. Serve hot.

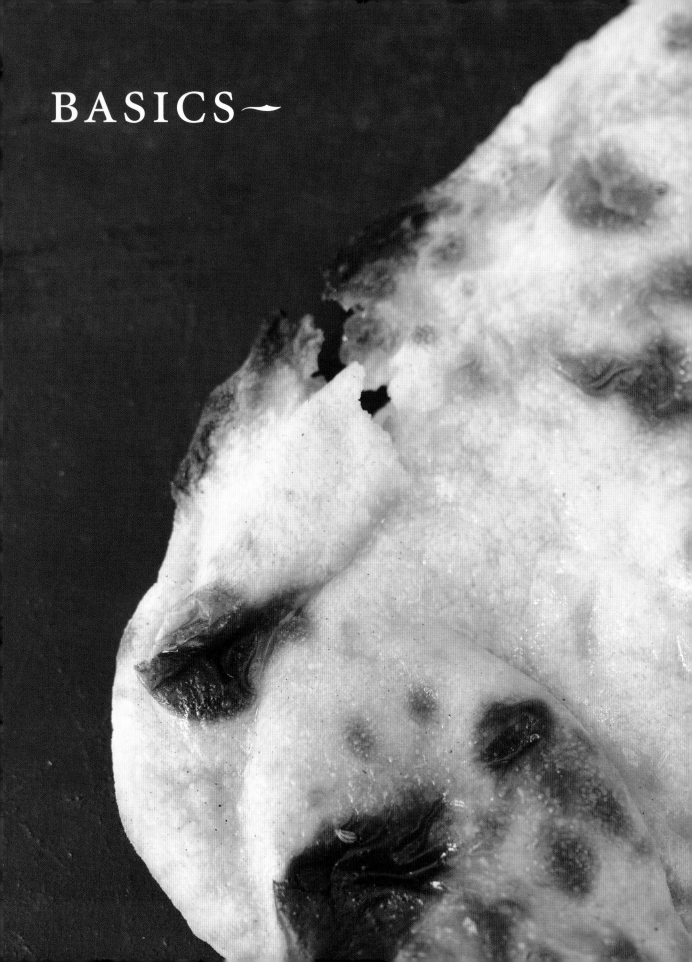

BASICS—

GARLIC PASTE

Peel a head of garlic and put it in a blender or mini food processor with 2–3 tablespoons of water and 1 tablespoon of vegetable oil. Blend to a paste. It will keep in the fridge for up to a week, or you can freeze it in ice-cube trays and then just take out a cube when you need it.

GINGER PASTE

Peel 300g fresh ginger, chop it roughly, then blend to a paste with 2 tablespoons of water in a mini food processor or a blender. Alternatively, grate the ginger very finely and mix with the water. You can freeze the paste in ice-cube trays, as for Garlic Paste above.

GINGER-GARLIC PASTE

This paste appears frequently in the recipes in this book, so it is very useful to have a stock in the fridge or freezer. To prepare, blend equal quantities of peeled garlic and fresh ginger with 10 per cent of their total weight in water, using a mini food processor or a blender. Store in a sealed container in the fridge. If you wish to keep it for more than a few days, add 5 per cent vegetable oil and 2 per cent lemon juice when you process it. Or you can freeze it in ice-cube trays, as for Ginger Paste, above.

MANGO PICKLE PASTE

I use this versatile ingredient a lot in my cooking. To make it, you simply need to buy a jar of good-quality mango pickle and either chop it very finely or blend it to a paste in a food processor.

DEEP-FRIED SLICED ONIONS

Deep-fried onions are used to add depth of flavour to dishes. Slice the onions very finely. Heat some vegetable oil to 180°C in a deep-fat fryer or a deep saucepan, add the onions and fry until crisp and brown. Drain thoroughly on kitchen paper to remove excess oil.

GARAM MASALA

30g black cardamom seeds
15g cloves
2.5cm piece of cinnamon stock
20g black cumin seeds
20g black peppercorns
a pinch of grated nutmeg (optional)

Garam masala is a spice mixture that is usually added towards the end of cooking. It is used in many dishes and contributes flavour and aroma.

Briefly roast the ingredients separately in a dry frying pan until they become aromatic. Leave to cool, then grind to a fine powder in a spice grinder or coffee grinder. Store the garam masala in an airtight container; it should keep for months.

FISH STOCK

MAKES 2 LITRES

1.5kg fish bones (preferably from
  white fish)
3 litres water
2 tablespoons vegetable oil
1 onion, roughly chopped
2 celery sticks, chopped
2 carrots, chopped
a sprig of thyme
2–3 sprigs of coriander
1–2 bay leaves
a small knob of fresh ginger
1 teaspoon fennel seeds
1 teaspoon coriander seeds
½ teaspoon black peppercorns
2 cloves

A neutral fish stock will work for the recipes in this book but if
you add spices, the stock will be much stronger and enhance
the flavour of the dish.

Put the fish bones and water into a large pan, bring to the boil
and simmer very gently for 15–20 minutes.

Meanwhile, heat the oil in another large pan, add the
vegetables, herbs and spices and sauté for a minute or so, until
the seeds pop. Strain the liquid from the other pan into the
vegetable and spice mixture, discarding the bones. Simmer for
about 30 minutes, until reduced to 2 litres, then strain through
a fine sieve and leave to cool. Store in the fridge or freezer.

VARIATIONS

Shellfish stock
Make as for Fish Stock, substituting prawn, lobster or
langoustine shells for the fish bones.

Saffron stock
After straining the stock, add a pinch of saffron strands, then
return it to the heat and simmer for 2–3 minutes.

MALVANI MASALA

10 dried red chillies
50g coriander seeds
5 cloves
1 tablespoon fennel seeds
½ teaspoon cumin seeds
½ teaspoon caraway seeds
1 black cardamom pod
5cm piece of cinnamon stick
¼ teaspoon mustards seeds
½ teaspoon ground turmeric
¼ teaspoon asafoetida
½ nutmeg
1 star anise

Malvan is a small town in western India, famous for its fish dishes and spice blends. This versatile spice mix can be used in meat cookery as well.

Briefly roast the ingredients separately in a dry frying pan until they become aromatic. Leave to cool, then grind to a fine powder in a spice grinder or coffee grinder. Store in an airtight container; it will keep for months.

MADRAS SPICE POWDER

10 curry leaves
1 teaspoon ground turmeric
2 teaspoons coriander seeds
1 teaspoon cumin seeds
2.5cm piece of cinnamon stick
3 cloves
1 dried red chilli
½ bay leaf
¼ teaspoon fenugreek seeds
½ teaspoon allspice berries
½ teaspoon black peppercorns

This spice mix will make life easier for novice cooks. I have taken most of the common spices used in southern India and created this blend to give a flavour of the south. In reality, there are different blends for different dishes. This one will get you started, however, and then you can create individual spice blends later.

Grind all the spices together and store in an airtight container. Use within 4 weeks.

SAMBHAR POWDER

1 tablespoon bengal gram dal (urad dal)
2 teaspoons coriander seeds
1 teaspoon cumin seeds
½ teaspoon fenugreek seeds
1 teaspoon ground turmeric
½ teaspoon asoefetida
1 teaspoon mustard seeds
6 dried red chillies
a sprig of dried curry leaves
2 tablespoons grated fresh coconut
  (see page 216)
8 black peppercorns

Typically, sambhar powder includes roasted lentils, coriander seeds, dried red chilli, fenugreek seeds and curry leaves. Regional variations may also include other spices, such as mustard seeds, cumin, black pepper and cinnamon.

Roast each of the ingredients separately in a dry frying pan until aromatic. Leave to cool, then grind to a powder in a spice grinder or coffee grinder. The powder will keep for months in an airtight container.

SPICY TOMATO CHUTNEY

1 tablespoon vegetable oil
½ teaspoon cumin seeds
2 green cardamom pods
1 bay leaf
2.5cm piece of cinnamon stick
1 dried red chilli
1kg tomatoes, chopped
1 teaspoon ground coriander
½ teaspoon ground turmeric
¼ teaspoon garam masala
1 teaspoon chopped fresh ginger
250g brown sugar or palm sugar
250ml white wine vinegar or white
  vinegar
sea salt

This is a favourite of mine – an all-time hit.

Heat the oil in a large saucepan, add the cumin, cardamom, bay leaf, cinnamon and red chilli and sauté for 1–2 minutes, until the spices splutter. Add the chopped tomatoes and cook for 2–3 minutes, then add the ground spices, ginger and some salt. Cook for 3–4 minutes, then add the sugar and vinegar and bring to the boil, stirring to dissolve the sugar. Simmer for about 45 minutes, stirring often, until the chutney is thick enough to coat the back of the spoon. Remove from the heat and leave to cool. Keep in the fridge for up to a week, or store in sealed sterilised jars and consume within 2 months.

GOOSEBERRY CHUTNEY

2 tablespoons vegetable oil
2 teaspoons Panch Phoran
  (see page 217)
1 teaspoon fennel seeds
½ teaspoon cumin seeds
2 cloves
1 black cardamom pod
1 onion, sliced
1 tablespoon Ginger-Garlic Paste
  (see page 202)
½ teaspoon red chilli powder
1 teaspoon ground coriander
½ teaspoon ground turmeric
200g fresh (or canned) gooseberries
50g palm sugar (or white or brown
  sugar)
50ml white wine vinegar
500ml water

I love this chutney. It goes well with roasted and cured meats as well as fish, and works wonders as a relish with salads.

Heat the oil in a pan, add the whole spices and cook for a minute until they crackle. Add the sliced onion, fry till golden brown, then add the ginger-garlic paste and cook for 2 minutes. Stir in the ground spices and gooseberries, followed by the sugar, vinegar and water. Bring to the boil and simmer until the chutney is thick. Remove from the heat and leave to cool.

CORIANDER AND PEANUT CHUTNEY

SERVES 4

100g coriander leaves
50g mint leaves
35g roasted peanuts
10g fresh ginger, finely chopped
1 green chilli, chopped
2 tablespoons lemon juice
1 teaspoon salt
1 tablespoon water

This could be considered the Indian equivalent of pesto. Use for flavouring marinades and sauces or to finish dishes by adding a couple of spoonfuls at the end of cooking.

Blend all the ingredients together in a food processor or blender to make a paste, then correct the seasoning.

TAMARIND CHUTNEY

SERVES 4

200g Tamarind Pulp (see page 218)
70g jaggery (or dark molasses sugar)
4 garlic cloves, chopped
1 teaspoon ground ginger
1 teaspoon fennel seeds
1 teaspoon cumin seeds
1 teaspoon black salt (if unavailable, use ordinary sea salt)
2 red chillies, left whole
½ teaspoon black peppercorns

Tamarind chutney can be cooked or raw, but I prefer this cooked version.

Put all the ingredients in a large pan, cover with water and bring to the boil. Simmer gently, stirring occasionally, for 15–20 minutes, until the mixture is fairly thick. Remove from the heat and leave to cool, then pass it through a fine sieve.

MINT AND CORIANDER CHUTNEY

SERVES 4–6

200g mint leaves
100g coriander leaves
20g fresh ginger, roughly chopped
2 green chillies
2 tablespoons lemon juice
100g Greek-style yoghurt
1 teaspoon chaat masala
sea salt

This chutney goes well with fish, meats and vegetables and is particularly good with fried and barbecued food. Use it as freely as ketchup.

Put the herbs in a food processor or blender with the ginger, chillies and lemon juice and process until smooth. Stir in the yoghurt, chaat masala and some salt to taste. Store in the fridge.

TOMATO-GINGER CHUTNEY

SERVES 4

2 tablespoons vegetable oil
½ teaspoon cumin seeds
½ teaspoon onion seeds
2 tablespoons chopped fresh ginger
200g tomatoes, chopped
¼ teaspoon red chilli powder
½ teaspoon ground coriander
50ml white wine vinegar
50g caster sugar
sea salt

My father taught me how to make this chutney. It was his favourite. Its light flavours work well in all seasons.

Heat the oil in a saucepan, add the onion and cumin seeds and sauté over a medium heat for a minute or so until they pop. Add the ginger and sauté for 1–2 minutes, then add the tomatoes. Cook for 1–2 minutes, then stir in the remaining ingredients. Simmer for 8–10 minutes, until the tomatoes have cooked down to form a sauce. Remove from the heat and leave to cool.

PASSION FRUIT AND SWEET CHILLI SAUCE

SERVES 4

200ml passion fruit purée
½ teaspoon red chilli flakes
80g caster sugar
1½ teaspoons cornflour mixed to a
   paste with 3 tablespoons water
sea salt

Here the tanginess of passion fruit and the heat of chilli are balanced with sugar. It's a fabulous chutney that works well with seafood and meats, and can also be used in a vinaigrette to dress salads. Passion fruit purée is available in sachets from some supermarkets and frozen from specialist shops, or online from www.merchant-gourmet.com.

Put all the ingredients except the cornflour paste into a pan and bring to the boil, stirring to dissolve the sugar. Stir in the cornflour paste and simmer for a few minutes, until the sauce thickens. Remove from the heat and leave to cool.

FRESH TOMATO AND CORIANDER CHUTNEY

SERVES 4

200g tomatoes, chopped
½ teaspoon finely chopped fresh
   ginger
¼ small green chilli, chopped
½ teaspoon cumin seeds, toasted in a
   dry frying pan and then ground to
   a powder
2 tablespoons lemon juice
1 tablespoon olive oil
1 garlic clove, chopped
3 tablespoons chopped coriander leaves
sea salt

I love this chutney with summer lunches. It's a great quick accompaniment to a light meal and fits in with whatever you have on the table. It also works well as a dip with some crusty bread.

Put all the ingredients in a food processor and pulse until finely chopped but not puréed.

SWEET YOGHURT CHUTNEY

SERVES 4

1 tablespoon vegetable oil
½ teaspoon mustard seeds
3 curry leaves, chopped
¼ teaspoon ground turmeric
½ teaspoon finely chopped fresh
  ginger
200g Greek-style yoghurt
1 tablespoon honey

This chutney makes an excellent dip with seafood and vegetable fritters, or bhajis. Just make sure that the mustard seeds pop open while sautéing, as this brings all their flavour out into the oil.

Heat the oil in a small pan, add the mustard seeds and curry leaves and sauté until the seeds pop. Add the turmeric and ginger and cook for 1–2 minutes. Stir in the yoghurt and honey, then transfer immediately to a bowl to cool.

SPICY INDIAN KETCHUP

2 tablespoons vegetable oil
1 red chilli, left whole
1 tablespoon chopped garlic
200ml tomato ketchup
1 tablespoon lemon juice
4 tablespoons water
2 spring onions, thinly sliced

I was bored with ketchup out of a bottle, I needed more flavour – so I made this one up.

Heat the oil in a saucepan, add the red chilli and garlic and sauté until the garlic turns light brown. Add the tomato ketchup and lemon juice and simmer for 2–3 minutes. Add the water and simmer for 2 minutes. Remove from the heat and stir in the sliced spring onions. Leave to cool, then store in the fridge. It should keep for 2 weeks.

KUMQUAT CHUTNEY

SERVES 4

100g kumquats, sliced
30g palm sugar (or white or brown
  sugar)
20ml white vinegar
½ teaspoon cumin seeds, lightly
  toasted in a dry frying pan and then
  crushed
½ teaspoon coriander seeds, toasted in
  a dry frying pan and then crushed
1 red chilli, left whole
1 teaspoon dried melon seeds (or
  sunflower seeds)
1 teaspoon sea salt

The sweet skin of kumquats gives this chutney a beautiful flavour and goes well with the toasted cumin.

Put all the ingredients in a small, heavy-based pan, bring to a simmer and cook gently for about half an hour, until the mixture has a thick, chutney-like consistency. Leave to cool before serving.

RAITA

SERVES 4

200g Greek-style yoghurt
½ teaspoon cumin seeds, toasted in a
  dry frying pan
a pinch of crushed black pepper
½ teaspoon lime juice (optional)
sea salt

This is the basic recipe for raita. You could flavour it with chopped cucumber, coriander, mint or other herbs, if you like.

Whisk all the ingredients together and chill until required.

VARIATION
Onion Raita
Add 2–3 tablespoons finely chopped red onion to the raita.

BOILED RICE

SERVES 4

200g basmati rice
sea salt

Indians love rice and breads and both can be present at the same meal. I prefer plain boiled rice with Indian food, as it provides a great background against which the other flavours can shine.

Tip the rice into a sieve and rinse under the cold tap, then leave to soak in a bowl of cold water for 5-10 minutes. Bring 2 litres of salted water to the boil in a saucepan. Drain the rice, add to the boiling water and simmer for 5-8 minutes, until just tender. Drain and keep warm until required, or serve immediately.

VARIATION
Chutney Rice
Stir 4 tablespoons of Mint and Coriander Chuntney (see page 207) into the cooked rice.

MASALA MASH

SERVES 4

450g potatoes, peeled and cut into
  chunks
1 tablespoon vegetable oil
½ teaspoon mustard seeds
6–8 curry leaves, chopped
½ teaspoon ground turmeric
½ tablespoon butter
sea salt

Mashed potato is served as a vegetable rather than a starch in India. This mash is very southern Indian in character.

Cook the potatoes in boiling salted water until tender, then drain. Pass through a potato ricer (or a sieve) to make a purée.

Heat the oil in a pan, add the mustard seeds and curry leaves and sauté for a minute or two, until the seeds pop. Add the turmeric and sauté for 30 seconds, then stir in the potatoes and butter. Mix well and cook, stirring, over a medium heat for 3–5 minutes. Season with salt and serve immediately.

FISH – INDIAN STYLE

CHAPATTIS

250g wholewheat flour
1 teaspoon salt
150ml water
ghee or butter for smearing the bread
   (optional)

Chapatti bread is one of the basics in any Indian household. It has various names, including *roti* and *phulka*, and is always made with wholewheat flour. It's impossible to give an exact quantity for the water, as the absorption qualities of different flours can vary quite considerably; the best thing to do is aim for a soft but not sticky dough.

Sift the flour and salt into a bowl, add about two-thirds of the water and mix until smooth. Slowly add enough of the remaining water to give a soft dough, then turn out on to a work surface and knead for a few minutes, until smooth and elastic. Return to the bowl and leave to rest for 15 minutes, covered with a damp cloth.

Divide the dough into 10–12 pieces, shape them into balls and dust with a little flour. Flatten each ball with the palm of your hand and then your fingers, pressing it out on a floured surface, and then roll out into a 12cm disc.

Heat a flat griddle or *tawa* and place a chapatti on it. Cook over a low heat for 1–2 minutes, until it starts to dry out and bubbles appear on the surface. Turn the chapatti over and cook the other side for 1–2 minutes. Both sides should be speckled with brown.

Remove from the griddle and hold over a gas flame with the help of tongs for a few seconds, until the bread puffs up (if you don't have a gas hob, you can put the bread in a very hot frying pan). Remove from the flame, brush with a little ghee or butter, if liked, and serve hot. If you need to make the breads in advance, keep them wrapped in a cloth and store in a container.

NAAN

This is the classic teardrop-shaped bread of northern India, leavened with yeast and traditionally cooked in a tandoor oven.

SERVES 4

1 tablespoon dried yeast
1 teaspoon sugar
150ml warm milk
450g strong white flour
2 teaspoons sea salt
2 tablespoons yoghurt
3 tablespoons melted butter
2 tablespoons poppy seeds
1 tablespoon sesame seeds

Stir the yeast and sugar into the warm milk and set aside for 20 minutes, until frothy.

Sift the flour and salt into a mixing bowl and add the yoghurt, 2 tablespoons of the melted butter and the yeast mixture. Mix together to make a soft dough, then turn out on to a floured work surface and knead for 8–10 minutes, until smooth and elastic. Return to the bowl and leave in a warm place, covered with a damp cloth, for 1–2 hours, until doubled in size.

Divide the dough into 8 pieces, shape them into balls and leave to rest in a warm place for 10 minutes. Roll out each ball into a circle and then pull out one side to make a teardrop shape.

Mix together the poppy seeds, sesame seeds and remaining melted butter and spread them over the naan. Place on baking sheets and bake in an oven preheated to 220°C/Gas Mark 7 for 4–5 minutes, until brown specks appear on the surface. If the breads are not brown enough, put them under a preheated grill for a minute or so.

PARATHAS

These breads are very similar to chapattis but are enriched by layering with ghee or butter and then folded into various shapes, according to the region. In the Punjab, they are usually round or triangular, whereas in Uttar Pradesh they are square. Parathas are generally served for breakfast, with a vegetable curry or pickles and yoghurt.

250g wholewheat flour
1 teaspoon sea salt
150ml water
3 tablespoons ghee or melted butter

Prepare the dough as for chapattis, above, and leave to rest for 15 minutes, covered with a damp cloth.

Divide the dough into 5–6 pieces, shape them into balls and dust with a little flour. Flatten each ball with the palm of your hand and then your fingers, pressing it out on a floured surface, and then roll out into a 12cm disc. Brush a thin layer of ghee or butter on top and sprinkle with a little flour, then fold the disc in half. Apply another thin layer of ghee or butter and sprinkle a little more flour over it, then fold in half once more to form a triangle. Press the triangle of dough firmly and roll out with a rolling pin, maintaining the shape.

Bake the breads on a flat griddle as for chapattis. Once they are speckled with brown, brush both sides with ghee or butter and cook for another 30 seconds or so per side, until golden brown. Serve hot.

VARIATION
Add 1 teaspoon of ajwain or cumin seeds to make *ajwaini* or *jeera* parathas.

POORIS

These North Indian breads are deep-fried until soft and puffy. You can eat them plain or stuff them with various fillings, such as the prawn one on page 44.

250g wholewheat flour
1 teaspoon sea salt
2 tablespoons vegetable oil
about 125ml water
vegetable oil for deep-frying

Sift the flour and salt into a bowl and add the oil. Gradually mix in enough water to make a smooth, stiff dough. Turn out on to a floured work surface and knead for a few minutes, until smooth and elastic. Return to the bowl, cover with a damp cloth and leave to rest for 30 minutes.

Briefly knead the dough again, then divide it into 20 pieces for large pooris, 40 for small ones. Shape into balls and roll each one out on a lightly floured work surface into a 7.5cm disc for large pooris, or a 3–4cm disc for small ones. Prick them lightly with a fork, so they stay crisp and don't rise.

Heat the oil for deep-frying to 180–190°C in a deep-fat fryer, a wok or a deep saucepan. Deep-fry the pooris, a few at a time, for 1–3 minutes, depending on size, until they puff up. Turn and cook for a minute longer, then remove and drain on kitchen paper. Serve hot.

glossary

AJWAIN SEEDS

Also known as ajowan or carom, these pungent seeds are related to caraway, though their taste is more reminiscent of thyme. They are often confused with lovage seeds – even some dictionaries mistakenly state that ajwain comes from the lovage plant. Ajwain seeds are considered essential for fish cookery in northern India.

BLACK GRAM LENTILS

Known in India as *urad dal*, these protein-rich pulses are usually sold hulled and split, when, confusingly, they are creamy white in colour, since it is only the skin that is black. The whole black lentils are harder to digest but can be delicious when cooked well.

CHAAT MASALA

Chaat masala is a powdered spice mix, typically consisting of dried mango powder, cumin, coriander, dried ginger, dried mint, asafoetida, black salt, ordinary salt and red and black pepper. Used as a salad seasoning, it is served on a small metal plate or in a dried banana leaf bowl at chaat, or salad carts, in India. You should be able to find it in Asian food shops.

COCONUT

Fresh coconuts are used a great deal on the coast in India. To extract the flesh from a coconut, push a skewer through one of the three 'eyes' to make a hole and then drain off the liquid (this can be strained and used in drinks). Next crack open the nut – the easiest way is to tap it round its circumference with a hammer, about a third of the way down from the 'eyes'. Break the nut into chunks and cut out the white flesh with a small, sharp knife. Remove the thin brown skin, then grate the flesh.

Coconut milk is made from the flesh and should not be confused with the liquid inside the coconut. To prepare coconut milk, soak 500g grated fresh coconut in 300ml lukewarm water for 30 minutes, then whiz in a blender on high speed for a few minutes. Strain the mixture through a sieve lined with a piece of muslin. It should yield about 250ml milk. This first extraction is known as thick coconut milk. You can then go on to make thin coconut milk by soaking the residue from the first extraction in 300ml lukewarm water and repeating the process.

Canned coconut milk is readily available and makes an acceptable substitute for fresh in most cases.

COCONUT VINEGAR

Coconut vinegar is made from tuba, the sap of the coconut tree. A 'tuba collector' climbs up the tree and clips the stem that holds the flowers and baby coconuts, then a collection vessel is hung from the tree and the stem placed so the sap will run into it. Every day a collector travels from treetop to treetop on bamboo poles to collect the sap from each tree. Coconut vinegar can be hard to find in the UK. If necessary, substitute white wine vinegar.

CURRY LEAVES

These small, slender, highly aromatic leaves come from the Murraya koenigii tree, which grows in hilly regions of India. They are used as a herb, much like bay leaves, in Indian and Sri Lankan cooking, especially in curries containing fish or coconut milk. Although they have a short shelf life when fresh, they may be stored in the freezer for quite some time. Curry leaves are also available dried, though the taste and aroma are inferior.

DRIED FENUGREEK LEAF POWDER

Fenugreek leaves taste very different from fenugreek seeds and the two are not interchangeable. Dried fenugreek leaf powder is available from Asian food shops, or you can grind your own dried fenugreek leaves in a spice grinder or pestle and mortar.

DRIED MANGO POWDER

Also known as amchoor, this is made by drying slices of green, unripe mango and then powdering them. Tangy and sour, it is used to flavour sauces and salad dressings.

GARAM MASALA

This blended spice powder is usually added to dishes towards the end of cooking. The recipe varies according to the region but typically it contains pepper, cumin, cinnamon, cloves and cardamom. Garam masala is available in supermarkets and Asian shops – or you can make your own (see page 202).

GRAM FLOUR

This fine, pale yellow flour is made from ground chickpeas and has an excellent nutty flavour. Also known as besan, it is used in breads, pancakes and in batters for coating fish and other foods.

PALM SUGAR AND JAGGERY

Palm sugar is made from the sap of various palm trees, such as date and coconut, while jaggery is a dark, unrefined sugar from the sugar cane plant. Loosely known as gur, palm sugar and jaggery are largely interchangeable in Indian cooking.

PANCH PHORAN

Panch phoran is a Bengali spice mix consisting of equal quantities of five strongly flavoured spices: fennel seeds, fenugreek seeds, onion seeds, cumin seeds and radhuni or mustard seeds. It's available in Asian shops or you can mix your own.

PANDANUS LEAVES

These bright green, spear-shaped leaves come from the screwpine tree in Asia and are often used to flavour rice or curry dishes. They have a gentle, slightly nutty flavour.

ROASTED CHANNA LENTILS

Channa dal, or yellow split peas, are the most commonly used pulse in India. The whole yellow peas can be roasted until they puff up and split open. The husk is then discarded and the lentils are split and sold as roasted channa dal. These lentils are sold in powdered form in East India, under the name, *sattu*, and are used as a filling for breads or for making a refreshing drink on hot summer days.

ROASTED MOONG LENTILS

Moong, or mung, lentils are native to India and are quick to cook and easy to digest. They are traditionally combined with rice in *kichri*, the Indian equivalent of kedgeree. You will find them plain or roasted in most Asian shops.

TAMARIND

Tamarind consists of the long, dark brown pods of the tropical tamarind tree and is popular in Indian cooking as a souring agent. Ready-prepared tamarind paste is available but I find that it can taste bitter and metallic once heated. Better to prepare your own, from the dried, compressed blocks of tamarind pods available in Asian shops. Break up a 200g pack, put it in a bowl and soak in about 400ml hot water for 20 minutes, until softened. Using your fingers, mix the pods with the water, which will thicken to a pulp. Strain through a sieve into a bowl, pressing to extract as much flavour as possible. It will keep in the fridge for 2–3 weeks or can be frozen. If you want a milder tamarind flavour, dilute the pulp with water.

TOASTING AND GRINDING SPICES

Whole spices are often toasted before use to intensify their flavour. Put them in a dry, heavy-based frying pan over a medium heat and toast until they crackle and become aromatic, stirring occasionally or shaking the pan to prevent burning. Once toasted, spices lose their flavour quickly, so always toast just before using.

To grind spices, pound them in a pestle and mortar for the best flavour, or use a spice grinder, coffee grinder or mini food processor.

*in*Dex

WITH THANKS TO:

SRK – my Dad, for being my inspirational hero
Jon Croft – for giving me the opportunity to write this book
David Loftus – for lively photography and support
Jane Middleton – for putting up with my slow pace on editing
Meg Avent – for her commission
Matt Inwood – for test eating each and every recipe and, of course, for beautiful design
Saurv Nath – my assistant chef, for testing and cooking the recipes
Sunil Ghai – chef at Ananda Restaurant, Dublin, for a huge contribution to the recipes
Balaji Balachender – head chef, Benares
Jitin Joshi – executive chef, Vatika
Naveen Bhatia, Jun Tanaka, Sriram Kailasam, Avijit Gosh
James Bulmer – my agent, for making this book happen

Deepti, Amisha and Arjun –
my lovely family, for putting up with me
during the creation of this book and
missing out on lots of family days out
– I will try to make it up to you all